VOGUE ON
YVES SAINT LAURENT

Natasha Fraser-Cavassoni

ABRAMS IMAGE
New York

At home in Marrakech, Yves Saint Laurent models his
new ready-to-wear line, Rive Gauche Pour Homme.
Photograph by Patrick Lichfield, 1969.

page one Model Carrie Nygren in Rive Gauche's black
double-breasted jacket and mid-calf skirt with long-
sleeved white blouse; styled by Grace Coddington,
photographed by Guy Bourdin, 1975.

previous page Linda Evangelista wears an ostrich-
feathered couture slip dress inspired by Saint Laurent's
favourite dancer, Zizi Jeanmaire. Photograph by Patrick
Demarchelier, 1987.

"CHRISTIAN DIOR TAUGHT ME THE ESSENTIAL NOBILITY OF A COUTURIER'S CRAFT."

YVES SAINT LAURENT

DIOR'S DAUPHIN

In fashion history, Yves Saint Laurent remains the most influential designer of the latter half of the twentieth century. Not only did he modernize women's closets—most importantly introducing pants as essentials—but his extraordinary eye and technique allowed every shape and size to wear his clothes. "My job is to work for women," he said. "Not only mannequins, beautiful women, or rich women. But all women." True, he dressed the swans, as Truman Capote called the rarefied group of glamorous socialites such as Marella Agnelli and Nan Kempner, and the stars, such as Lauren Bacall and Catherine Deneuve, but he also gave tremendous happiness to his unknown clients across the world. Whatever the occasion, there was always a sense of being able to "count on Yves." It was small wonder that British *Vogue* often called him "The Saint" because in his 40-year career women felt protected and almost blessed wearing his designs.

Although the Paris-based couturier wished that he had invented denim jeans—describing them as "the most spectacular, the most practical, the most relaxed, and nonchalant," to *Vogue*'s Gerry Dryansky—he was behind such well-cut staples as the pea coat, the safari jacket, the trench coat, the pant suit, *Le Smoking* (the female tuxedo), and the introduction of black tights as the chic alternative to pale hosiery. Following in the footsteps of Coco Chanel, Saint Laurent was inspired by black, yet he was a superb colorist who with his bold choice of fabric knew how to brighten an outfit and flatter the complexion.

Helmut Newton said Saint Laurent inspired his "best fashion photos." His mythic portrait of Vibeke Knudsen wearing Le Smoking *on the rue Abriot appeared in* Vogue Paris *in 1975. The pairing of tailored pant suit and soft blouse typified Saint Laurent's masculine-feminine ambiguity.*

overleaf *Naomi Campbell, a frequent Saint Laurent model, photographed by Patrick Demarchelier in 1987 (left) as a haute-couture-clad showgirl—a favorite night-time look of the couturier's. Rive Gauche shirt, sunglasses, and jewelry (right), are exotically displayed on Marie Helvin, another Saint Laurent favorite, photographed by David Bailey in 1975.*

As a demonstration of *Vogue*'s attention to promising fashion talent, Saint Laurent had strong links with the magazine from the very start of his career and throughout. It was via *Vogue*'s Michel de Brunhoff that he met Christian Dior, his first and only boss. It was through the enthusiasm of *Vogue*'s Diana Vreeland that the American public became instantly sold on Rive Gauche, Saint Laurent's ready-to-wear line.

"A GOOD MODEL CAN ADVANCE FASHION BY TEN YEARS."

YVES SAINT LAURENT

Meanwhile, Helmut Newton's iconic *Smoking* portrait taken in 1975 and other memorable images by the likes of Richard Avedon, David Bailey, Guy Bourdin, and Irving Penn were first viewed within the pages of *Vogue*.

Saint Laurent epitomised the expression "highly strung." Pierre Bergé, his business partner and one-time lover, described him as being "born with a nervous breakdown." Still, whatever his mood—"I am a persistent depressive," he told British *Vogue*'s Lesley White—or mental state, Saint Laurent never lost his adoring fashion audience. The interest in his personal welfare never faded. Though viewed as "the king of couture" and one of the "great talents," Saint Laurent was seen as human, and he touched people by his vulnerability—no doubt because he seemed authentic, and had always dared to be different and romantic. His declaration that "for a woman to look beautiful all she needs is to be in the arms of the man she loves" demonstrated this. A poetic thought, it suggested that he cared about women beyond clothes: *Yves le Séducteur*—the designer who both seduced with his perfect proportions and with his person.

Lucienne Saint Laurent, photographed for British Vogue by Willy Rizzo in 1960 with "the irrepressibly pleased expression of someone whose son has just pulled off an immensely successful coup." To set off her dramatic colouring, she was wearing a turquoise cardigan suit, from Saint Laurent's couture collection for Christian Dior.

previous page *Carla Bruni photographed by Dewey Nicks in 1994, wearing Saint Laurent's short couture silk faille evening dress, highlighted with jewelry designed by Loulou de la Falaise.*

From an early age, adoring females surrounded the designer. Born on August 1st, 1936 in Oran, Algeria, Yves Henri Donat Mathieu-Saint-Laurent was the apple of his mother Lucienne's eye. Cherubic, with large blue eyes and wide, smiling mouth, he displayed none of the anguish that would later cloud his features. He was a happy and cherished *petit prince*. Two younger sisters—Michèle and Brigitte—were to follow. "I love my daughters, of course," Lucienne told *Vogue*'s Dryansky, "but for Yves, there's always been something very strong and very special."

'Women are intrinsically mysterious, veiled, enigmatic.'

YVES SAINT LAURENT

The Saint Laurent family led a privileged existence. "There were many lovely dinner parties at our comfortable house in town," he wrote, "and I can still see my mother, about to leave for a ball, come to kiss me goodnight, wearing a long dress of white tulle with pear-shaped white sequins." His father, who owned an insurance business as well as being involved in the occasional movie production, was descended from distinguished public servants who had fled Alsace, France, when the Germans took it as war booty in 1870. "One of my ancestors wrote the marriage contract between Napoleon and Josephine and was made a baron for it," Saint Laurent revealed. His mother's background was more complicated. Her parents—a Belgian engineer and his Spanish wife—had handed her over to an Aunt Renée, the wife of an affluent architect, living in Oran. No expense had been spared for Lucienne, referred to as *la gata* (the cat) owing to her sparkling green eyes, which were enhanced by her copper-colored hair. An early poster girl for her son's designs, there was nothing remotely provincial about her appearance, but there again, Oran, then part of the French Empire, was one of the largest ports on the Mediterranean. "Our world then was Oran, not Paris," wrote Saint Laurent. "Oran, a cosmopolis of trading people from all over … a town glittering in a patchwork of all colors under the sedate North African sun."

"The intense melting pot of lives I knew in Oran … marked me," he told *Vogue*'s Joan Juliet Buck. He recalled the warships and all the wartime uniforms. "People tried to have some glamour in their lives because they were close to death," he continued. He had an extraordinary artistic talent, evident from the age of three, which his mother encouraged. He enchanted his two sisters, amusing Brigitte with his witty caricatures of Oran's church-going public, and arranging "no adults allowed" couture fashion shows. Aware of his precocious talent, Saint Laurent was keen for acclaim. As he later confessed, "I had just blown out the candles for my ninth birthday cake when, with a second gulp of breath, I hurled my secret across a table surrounded by my loving relatives: 'My name will be written in fiery letters on the Champs-Elysées.'"

previous pages Illustrating Saint Laurent's sensual way with fur (left), Nancy Donahue sports Rive Gauche's suede coat, lined in squirrel with silver fox collar. Photograph by Eric Boman, 1980 Cindy Crawford wears Rive Gauche's one-sleeve silk top with tulip sarong (right), an example of Saint Laurent's fondness for an asymmetrical style. Photograph by Patrick Demarchelier, 1987.

His home life was imaginative and fun, but his school days, spent at the Collège du Sacré-Coeur, the Jesuit Catholic boarding school, were unmitigated hell. Extremely thin and fey-looking, an appearance emphasized by the tight jackets and ties that he chose to wear, Yves became the target for the macho boys in his class. "I wasn't like the other boys. I didn't conform. No doubt it was my homosexuality," he told *Le Figaro*, the French newspaper, in 1991. "And so they made me into their whipping boy. They beat me up and locked me in the toilets … As they bullied me, I would say to myself over and over again, 'One day, you'll be famous.'"

Saint Laurent never told his family about the daily attacks. Still, the very idea of them made him violently sick, every morning. Fortunately his keenness to create clothes for his mother—her dressmaker began to use his sketches—as well as his love of the movie theater and theater would outweigh the horror of his schooldays. A touring production of Molière's play *L'Ecole des Femmes*, directed by the actor Louis Jouvet with sets by Christian Bérard, led to Saint Laurent's viewing theatrical design as a professional option. Suddenly, all the 12-year-old could talk about was theater. His parents let him use an empty room for productions that he wrote, staged, and cast using his sisters and cousins as actors.

Passion for the stage did not stop the 17-year-old Saint Laurent entering the International Wool Secretariat fashion competition. It led to his winning third prize and going with his mother to Paris in the fall of 1953. Thanks to his father's contacts, he met Michel de Brunhoff, the celebrated editor of *Vogue Paris*. Noted for his relationships with designers like Elsa Schiaparelli and Christian Dior, de Brunhoff was in a position to help Saint Laurent in the fashion world. The young man's mix of creative authority and extreme fragility tended to induce assistance. Indeed, *Vogue*'s de Brunhoff was the first in a long line of influential people who were supportive of Saint Laurent.

"I came to Paris determined to burst out on the world, one way or another."

YVES SAINT LAURENT

De Brunhoff was insistent that his young protégé finish his baccalaureate exams. Saint Laurent followed his advice, and also entered the 1954 International Wool Secretariat competition that boasted 6,000 entrants. His black cocktail dress complete with a veil worn over the face won first prize, while a certain Karl Lagerfeld won best jacket category. A photograph captures the event. Fanciful as Saint Laurent appeared—"elegance is a dress too dazzling to wear twice," he had said when presenting his dress—he actually possessed tremendous self-worth backed up by an eerie instinct. The year before, he and his mother had been admiring the fashion finery along Paris's avenue Montaigne when Saint Laurent had suddenly looked up at Christian Dior's headquarters and announced, "Maman, it won't be long until I'm working in there."

To improve his couture technique, de Brunhoff encouraged Saint Laurent to attend Paris's best fashion school, the Ecole de la Chambre Syndicale de la Couture Parisienne. However, three months on, the 18-year-old was bored by the experience, no doubt because he was both professionally focused and had already learned so much from his mother's dressmaker. Concerned by his son's general apathy, Charles Mathieu-Saint-Laurent recontacted de Brunhoff, and Saint Laurent returned to the *Vogue Paris* offices and stunned de Brunoff and Edmonde Charles-Roux, the magazine's new Editor-in-Chief, with his latest batch of sketches. They strongly resembled Christian Dior's new A-Line designs, a collection that was still under wraps. Frantic calls were made to Monsieur Dior who, after meeting Saint Laurent, hired him on the spot. "Working with Christian Dior was, for me, the achievement of a miracle," Saint Laurent told Dryansky. "I had endless admiration for him."

The 18-year-old Yves Mathieu-Saint-Laurent wins first prize in the dress category of the International Wool Secretariat, December 1954. This cocktail dress, chosen from an entry of 6,000 anonymous sketches, indicates his instinct for balance. Since it closed with buttons on the right, the shoulder was left bare.

"I was torn between the theater and fashion. It was my meeting with Christian Dior that guided me toward fashion."

YVES SAINT LAURENT

Monique

da

Christian DIOR
Avenue Montaigne - PARIS-8ᵉ
Croquis Nº 37   16 JUIN

94
Christiane
Fidélia

Christian DIOR
30 Avenue Montaigne - PARIS-8ᵉ
13 JUIN 1960   Croquis Nº 103

Marthe
151
Christine

Christian DIOR

Berta

Christian DIOR

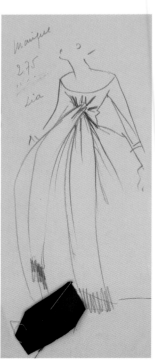

Monique
275
Lia

Christian Dior's New Look collection in February 1947 had made him France's most successful and famous couturier. His designs promoting a corseted hourglass torso as well as ankle-grazing hems—controversial owing to postwar fabric rationing—caused international fashion fever; Jean Cocteau, France's star poet and writer, was quoted as saying, "The 'New Look' is being given the importance of the atomic bomb." Within a few years, his clients consisted of A-List Hollywood sirens like Lauren Bacall, Marlene Dietrich, Ava Gardner, and Rita Hayworth as well as well-heeled members of society such as the Begum Aga Khan, Daisy Fellowes, Patricia Lopez-Willshaw, and the Duchess of Windsor.

Saint Laurent's couture drawings for the house of Christian Dior. Details like the tulip-shaped skirt and exposed back would feature in his own, future, fashion house. Throughout his career, few were not awed by the quick intelligence and fluid harmony behind his croquis *(fashion sketches).*

Rigorous about quality, the Christian Dior couture house was the perfect place for Saint Laurent to land because it would teach him about the importance of discipline in fashion. Brilliant as Saint Laurent was, he needed structure to calm and temper his creative imagination. Working alongside Monsieur Dior—a designer who would have his eternal respect both for succeeding and for being the friend of artists like Cocteau and his hero Christian Bérard—Saint Laurent would learn the essential basics. "Essential basics" that would underpin his future fashion house.

Christian Dior's seamlessly run couture house consisted of Jacques Rouët, the financial director; Suzanne Luling, who was in charge of the salon and *rendeuses* (the sales women); and three women who ran Dior's inner sanctum. Referred to as the "three fates" by the photographer Cecil Beaton, they were: Madame Raymonde Zehnacker who acted as the designer's alter ego; Madame Marguerite Carré, a technical expert who headed the ateliers; and Madame Mitzah Bricard, Dior's unofficial muse who created hats. Although fairly hierarchical, the "worker bee" atmosphere was civilized, and that stemmed from Dior himself. Modest and even-tempered, the couturier was rare in his world for being polite, industrious, and open-minded, though he was no pushover: employees were fired for not recognizing him, chewing gum, and other uncouth behavior.

Saint Laurent was wildly fortunate to fall into the fashion net of a true visionary who created one of the premier global brands, but there were mutual benefits. Saint Laurent had excellent taste and was full of fresh ideas and the latter was vital to Dior. After the excitement of the New Look, clients and buyers were expecting a surprise from Monsieur Dior every season. It was hard to keep up the momentum and the couturier depended on the assistants in his studio. According to Saint Laurent, he and Dior had a formal relationship. "We were very shy with each other and never had deep conversations," he told British *Vogue*'s White. "But he taught me many things, that frivolity is not a lack of intelligence ... and the rules of fashion. It was an incredible place to work."

Still, it has to be emphasized how painfully reticent and timid the bespectacled Saint Laurent was. Walking along the house's corridors, his tall, thin figure would press itself into the walls. His behavior either brought out maternal instincts—"you just wanted to hug and console him," said one Dior seamstress—or intrigued. Initially, Victoire, the Dior model, was reminded of a monk until the sultry brunette made a concerted effort to sit down and talk to Saint Laurent. "Then I was thoroughly charmed," she admits. And so began Saint Laurent's fabled way with women in the fashion world that continued throughout his life. Owing to his close relationship with his mother, he knew exactly how to enchant.

Marie-Hélène Arnaud, later Coco Chanel's muse, offers soignée attitude to Saint Laurent's "trapeze-style" tulle and silver-specked evening dress for Christian Dior, described by Vogue as "flaring out over the narrow sheath beneath." Photograph by Henry Clarke, 1958.

Nevertheless, it was a charm reserved for women. In Dior's studio, Saint Laurent refused to greet or speak to Yorn Michaelsen, a handsome fellow assistant who sat next to him. Michaelsen recognized that Saint Laurent was a genius' but behind the "shrinking violet" façade lurked "a monster." "He held a huge opinion of himself," recalls Michaelsen, as well as requiring "a court of admirers" led by the likes of Victoire. Of course, this exclusionary behavior was and remains fairly common practice in fashion but what is interesting is that Dior was aware of it and dismissed it as youthful silliness. A lesser designer might also have tried to block Saint Laurent's talent

or pretended that his sketches were his own. Instead, the thoroughly generous Dior—who forgave and accepted the foibles of the gifted—drew attention to his youthful assistant. Prior to collection time, the young protégé would deliver his sketches—mini marvels achieved back at his parent's home in Oran—that ultimately made up a large percentage of the show and, internally *chez Dior*, were recognized for doing so. Had Saint Laurent nursed doubts about his future, a meeting between his mother Lucienne and Dior confirmed that he was the designer's unofficial dauphin. The idea was that Saint Laurent would have several years to mature into the position. Unfortunately, only months later, Dior died of a heart attack, on October 24, 1957.

A much-loved figure and viewed as the hero who saved French couture, Dior was given a statelike funeral at Eglise Saint-Honoré-d'Eylau. It was noted that Saint Laurent was seated in a prominent pew, near famous couturiers like Cristóbal Balenciaga and Pierre Balmain, paying their respects, but there was a burning question: Would Marcel Boussac, who financed the house of Dior, pull the plug on the 60 million franc business? Among Dior's management, there were fears that Saint Laurent was simply too inexperienced to take over the reins. An official press conference was then conducted at Christian Dior's salon on avenue Montaigne. Jacques Rouët announced a creative team of four individuals who had all worked with Dior, namely Raymonde Zehnacker, Marguerite Carré, Mitzah Bricard, and Dior's 21-year-old assistant who still went by the name Yves Mathieu-Saint-Laurent.

Awkward as he seemed, Saint Laurent privately basked in the spotlight and enjoyed the drama of the occasion. Rushing to his parent's home in Oran, he later described himself "in a state of complete euphoria" when designing the collection because he sensed that he was "going to become famous." After three weeks, he returned with 1,000 sketches. There were a multitude of ideas but Zehnacker, Carré, and Bricard deftly edited them down to 178 looks.

On January 30, 1958 Yves Saint Laurent, as he became officially known having dropped the Mathieu, delivered his first Dior collection. It was called "Trapèze" owing to the main silhouette that was like a trapezium: fitted at the breast and then flared out below the knee. Light, breezy, and lacking an iota of Christian Dior's signature construction and padding, the presentation was hailed as a triumph.

Beckoned into Dior's Grand Salon, Saint Laurent received a standing ovation. "The reaction of joy and relief was terrific," reported British *Vogue*. "People cried, laughed, clapped and shook hands. For almost an hour no one would leave." The new star was then led up the stairs to the second floor's wrought iron balcony where Monsieur Dior famously used to take his bows. The image of Saint Laurent being cheered and clapped by cab drivers and passersby was caught on camera. The next morning, the newspaper sellers shouted, "Saint Laurent has saved France." It was news that was furthered by a fleet of glowing reviews.

Yves Saint Laurent, after his Christian Dior show in July 1960 with "cabine" models, Patricia, Laurence, Fidélia, Déborah, and Valérie. The couturier reveled in their company. Like his mentor Dior, he recognized that they were essential to his designs.

In Saint Laurent's opinion, he resembled a "studious schoolboy" during his Dior days but the French media used expressions like "sickly child," "shy and stooped," and "a fawn in the forest." And it is hard not to agree with Alicia Drake, the author of *The Beautiful Fall: Fashion, Genius and Glorious Excess in 1970s Paris* that, from the very beginning, "the image conjured up" of Saint Laurent was that of "victim in victory, of a youth sacrificed for fashion." "This would be the highly emotive vernacular that would stay with him and describe him throughout his career," she wrote. Indeed, whatever Saint Laurent did, tended to inspire protective feelings.

'Suddenly the house of Dior had taken
a real youth pill.'

SUSAN TRAIN, VOGUE

"I WORK, I DRAW A LOT.
I DON'T LET MYSELF BE INFLUENCED."

YVES SAINT LAURENT

FASHION'S NEW GENIUS

In the October 1960 issue, *Vogue* published a photograph of one of Yves Saint Laurent's final designs for the house of Dior. Taken by Irving Penn, it was a black crocodile jacket, trimmed with mink. Edgy and hip, it lacked the *jeune fille* sedateness of his "Trapèze" line and suggested that little Yves had grown up and rebelled. He had—by delivering the "Beat" collection, which was inspired by Juliette Gréco, the French singer and cool queen of Paris's beatnik scene. "This was the first collection in which I tried for poetic expression in my clothes," Saint Laurent wrote. "Social structures were breaking up. The street had a new pride, its own chic, and I found the street inspiring, as I would often again." Although the mostly black clothes sold well, the Dior management were appalled.

Unlike Christian Dior who was always prepared to take risks, Madame Raymonde and the others running his empire were fairly conservative. No doubt it explained both the hiring and secret holding onto the French designer Marc Bohan, in spite of Saint Laurent's initial success. Mature and predictable in style, Bohan was kept in London, just in case Dior's young Dauphin did not cut the mustard.

Early photographs of Saint Laurent, taken with Mesdames Raymonde, Marguerite, and Mitzah, suggest a polite young man in the company of his maiden aunts. Later ones, however, indicate more confidence, no doubt because he had branched out to design costumes for Roland Petit, the enfant terrible of the ballet world, and because he had a lover, the 27-year-old Pierre Bergé. Many books, many organized by Bergé, have described their tumultuous and extremely productive relationship. And since Bergé was a pugnacious force of nature next to the more elegant, retiring Saint Laurent, it might be presumed that Bergé is sounding his own trumpet. Nevertheless, the Napoleonic Bergé deserves recognition for his part in Saint Laurent's illustrious career because he always believed in the designer and fought for him tooth and nail, whatever the circumstances. Without Bergé, it is unlikely that Saint Laurent would have soared to such great heights.

In the Christian Dior salon, wearing his blouse blanche (white coat), Saint Laurent highlights the lines of his "Chicago" jacket. A leather stunner from his final Dior couture collection, the "soft and supple" piece was described by Vogue as "a glossy black crocodile jacket" edged with mink and crocodile bows.

overleaf Wilhelmina models a sand-colored wool fisherman's shirt jacket, an early iconic Saint Laurent couture piece, teamed with a "straight charcoal dress" and "brass beaver hat." Seeing it as strikingly innovative, Vogue referred to the top's "wind-ballooned back" and being "knotted saltily at front." Photograph by Irving Penn, 1962.

"A GARMENT IS HELD
ON BY ITS SHOULDERS
AND THE NAPE
OF THE NECK.
THAT IS THE MOST
IMPORTANT PART.
THIS IS HOW THE
GARMENT IS DRAPED."

YVES SAINT LAURENT

Saint Laurent was a fashion genius but he was an extremely neurotic thoroughbred who needed hand-holding in every single instance, and Bergé, who would regard him as the great love of his life, had both the intelligence and energy to cope with the couturier's demands.

Like *Vogue*'s Michel de Brunhoff and Christian Dior, Saint Laurent's former mentors, Bergé had an enduring respect for the arts. His passion for poets, writers, artists, and dancers was something that he always shared with Saint Laurent; it was a key and lasting element of their relationship. Although Bergé lacked a formal education—he had left home before obtaining his baccalaureate—propelled by personal ambition, he was determined to better himself. Without either the privilege of Saint Laurent's upbringing—his father was a tax inspector —or the added advantage of unconditional maternal love (his mother viewed him as "lazy and undecided"), Bergé had only one dream: to flee the provinces and "find freedom" in Paris. After various schemes such as journalism and secondhand book dealing, he started an eight-year affair with the respected and successful artist Bernard Buffet. He had done portraits of Dior and other notables and Bergé promoted Buffet as if he was the new Picasso. The first time Victoire, the model, saw Bergé, she could not believe his gall and pushiness. However, when they eventually became friends, she was seduced by his agile mind and charm.

Pierre Bergé, left, and Saint Laurent photographed by Pierre Boulat at their new couture house on rue Spontini. Snared between fittings, the couturier combs through technical details. Understaffed before the first couture collection, Bergé and he had to furiously multitask.

Bergé and Saint Laurent had met at a dinner given by Marie-Louise Bousquet, the *Harper's Bazaar* correspondent, in honor of Saint Laurent. For Bergé, it was *un coup de foudre*, love at first sight. Bergé was struck by Saint Laurent's romantic looks and vulnerability. "He was a strange, shy boy," he told British *Vogue*'s Lesley White. "He reminded me of a clergyman, very serious, very nervous." Bergé—a power animal, short and sexually virile rather than handsome—made his presence known at Dior, chatting up Suzanne Luling in the salon and demanding a chauffeur-driven car for Saint Laurent; having been friendly with Monsieur Dior, he was aware of a star couturier's entitlements. However, Bergé truly came into his element when Saint

pour Y. S. L.
Amicalement A. W. L.
62

Laurent was conscripted into the army in the summer of 1960. Saint Laurent reported for military duties and then had a nervous collapse. At first, he was sent to the Bégin military hospital and then incarcerated at Val-de-Grâce's military hospital, in the south of Paris. This was a torturous ordeal and lasted until mid-November 1960. Crazed types ran in and out of Saint Laurent's room, while he was put through a series of electric shock treatments as well as being force-fed unnecessarily heavy tranquilizers. When given his leave, Saint Laurent weighed 77 pounds (35 kilos). Although no one was meant to visit him, Bergé forced his way in and managed to get him released from hospital. He also broke the news that Marc Bohan had replaced Saint Laurent at Dior in October.

Devastating as the information was, Saint Laurent did not crumble. Becoming quite calm, he famously said: "There is no other solution, we have to open a couture house." It was bold, and yet another example of Saint Laurent's tremendous confidence in his own talent. Encouraged by Bergé he sued Dior for breach of contract and won 680,000 francs ($72,665) in damages. Bergé also sold his apartment and a few of his Bernard Buffet paintings. It was courageous, but Saint Laurent had become his passion and cause. The belligerent Bergé turned into Saint Laurent's guard dog. Promoting and protecting his lover's talent became a fundamental element of their partnership and gave it its enduring force.

Adolphe Jean-Marie Mouron, professionally known as Cassandre, designed the YSL logotype in 1961. Influenced by cubism and surrealism, Cassandre was known for the boldness of his typefaces, an essential ingredient for the three initials that needed to capture attention and travel the world.

For their office, Bergé rented two rooms on the rue la Boétie in the 8th arrondissement and hired the graphic artist Cassandre to design the iconic YSL logo. Victoire was also taken on board, officially doubling as mannequin and *directrice de couture*, but really being there to console Saint Laurent and counteract his gloomy, and daily, declarations of "I am done for ... I'm finished." Despite Saint Laurent's doubts, Bergé's valiant efforts and tireless networking secured an American backer in the form of Jesse Mack Robinson, a self-made millionaire car dealer from Atlanta. On December 4, 1961, they moved to larger, temporary premises and opened the house of Yves Saint Laurent. The event was marked by an article in *Paris Match*, which was edited by Roger Thérond, Victoire's husband. Photographs show Saint Laurent posing in front of bolts of fabric while the former Dior star model, typical for the period, was smoking with one hand and telephoning with another. "The starkness of the setting and the dramatic composition of the photograph express the huge pressure Yves was under to pull the rabbit out of the hat," wrote Alicia Drake in *The Beautiful Fall*. Even so, the article stirred interest and was the perfect follow-up to the *Paris Match* teaser published in August 1961 under the title of "Deux Parisiennes semblent porter du Yves Saint Laurent" (Two Parisians appear to be wearing Yves Saint Laurent) showing Victoire and Zizi Jeanmaire, the famous dancer, who relied on Saint Laurent for her stage costumes.

Saint Laurent's plaid wool and gold buttoned suit with, said Vogue, "small pointed collar ... sleeves mounted low and squarely," photographed by William Klein in 1962. It displayed the conventional approach, apparent in his early collections; a modern element offering mild contrast was "the tied leather belt."

Pierre Boulat, the French photographer, was hired to record the action prior to Saint Laurent's very first collection. Boulat caught Saint Laurent "standing, sitting, kneeling, crouching to correct a fabric or drape a length of cloth." Wearing a plain white cotton coat that prevented distraction, allowing him to focus on the model and the outfit's fabric, Saint Laurent is in a swirl of action whether spreading out his sketches, checking on the length of skirt, holding up embroidery to an evening dress, trying a hat out on Victoire, and inspecting costume jewelry, via his long tapered fingers. One portrait illustrates his anguish. Seated at his desk with a simple light over his head and the year's cardboard calendar perched behind his chair, Saint Laurent covers his glasses and face with his hands. Meanwhile, Bergé kept to his office, arranging the launch on January 29, 1962 at an *hôtel particulier* on the rue Spontini in the 16th arrondissement.

In the salon, no-nonsense wooden chairs replaced the little gold ones so reminiscent of stuffy couture occasions, while the appearance of Helena Rubenstein, the makeup magnate, Jacqueline de Ribes,

the society hostess, and Lee Radziwill, the socialite sister of Jackie Kennedy, added to the atmosphere. The collection was judged a hit by Saint Laurent's friends, such as Jeanmaire and novelist Françoise Sagan, although some felt it was fairly conformist, as it consisted of wool day suits, cocktail dresses, and Raj coats. British *Vogue*, on the other hand, found Saint Laurent's suits "surprisingly, unbeat," drawing attention to the "neat jacket with set-in sleeves, a slight concave scoop to the front, cropped to show an inch or two of blouse" and the skirt "wrapped like a sarong with a soft centre fold." They also mentioned the "stark, nun-like simplicity" of his black dress, made of black soufflé crepe that contrasted with "the ruffles and frilleries" viewed at Lanvin, Laroche, and other French fashion houses. And *Vogue* across the Atlantic referred to "beauties … that will surely be seen at elegant parties in New York, Paris, London, Rome—over and over again."

Vogue presented "Yves Saint Laurent's dress and pullover partnership" on Jean Shrimpton, photographed by David Bailey in 1963. Suggesting future flair, the "dead simple" fitted wool jersey dress with short sleeves and "curled collar" contrast with the roomy, sailorlike tweed top.

The day after Saint Laurent's show, couture clients had rushed in, ordering six or seven outfits. The first person was Patricia Lopez-Willshaw who chose a jet-encrusted evening gown. This was a serious compliment; Lopez-Willshaw was a recognized international *grande dame* of fashion, noted for wearing Schiaparelli and Dior. Her confidence in Saint Laurent would inspire others to follow suit.

I n the Parisian haute couture world of the early sixties, society played a key element; hostesses could encourage interest in designers by inviting them to their homes. Since Bergé and Saint Laurent knew *les règles du jeu* (the rules of the game), were cultured and *au courant*, they became socially in demand. What is admirable about Bergé and Saint Laurent is that they never hid their homosexuality, during an era when many others in fashion did. And their bohemian attitude and lifestyle attracted Parisian powerhouses like Marie-Hélène de Rothschild, the wife of a millionaire banker; Hélène Rochas, the exquisite widow of Marcel Rochas who ran his fragrance empire; and Charlotte Aillaud, the sister of Juliette Gréco and the wife of a prominent architect. The erudite Bergé knew how to flatter and was

skilled at presenting Saint Laurent as the new "boy genius" in the fashion world, and the charismatic designer played the role to the hilt. At ease in female company, he quietly charmed women with his good looks and intelligent observations about their appearance.

Saint Laurent and Bergé also won over key members of the media. John Fairchild, then running *Women's Wear Daily*, was smitten, as was the *New York Herald Tribune*'s Eugenia Sheppard and Diana Vreeland, who would join *Vogue* later that year. Recalling her first meeting with Saint Laurent, Vreeland described, "a thin, thin, tall boy" who was "something within himself ... He struck me right away as a person with enormous inner strength, determination ... and full of secrets. I think his genius is in letting us know one of his secrets from time to time."

Saint Laurent's designs grew more confident and youthful with each season. *Vogue* referred to his second collection as "a glittering tour de force, greeted with the special kind of emotional fervor reserved for such occasions." He introduced a chic softness, tiered dresses, and tunics with easy sleeves and bold buttons as well as thigh-high boots. Fairchild referred to his 1964 fall/winter show as "the most beautiful collection" he had ever seen in Paris, "marking the return to gracious, refined clothes."

Then, in the summer of 1965, Saint Laurent unveiled his Mondrian collection. In this iconic collection, Saint Laurent used reproductions of the Dutch artist's paintings on straight jersey dresses. Cutting a sharp, modern figure, with its excellent use of abstraction, perfect proportions, and choice of crisp white jersey, the Mondrian dress was hailed as the dress of tomorrow. The Mondrian made the *Vogue Paris* September cover—a first for Saint Laurent's fashion house—and *Vogue* photographed the hit dress on the long limbs of Veruschka, the German supermodel. "Contrary to what people may think, the severe lines of the paintings matched the female body very well," Saint Laurent later said. The Mondrian dress—an unforgettable classic—typified his scene-stealing designs by

"THE MASTERPIECE OF THE TWENTIETH CENTURY IS A MONDRIAN."

YVES SAINT LAURENT

Saint Laurent's Mondrian couture dress was his first design to have instant international appeal. Vogue mentioned the "jersey rectangles," the "blocks of color laid on like fresh paint," and the "elongated proportions." "Bottle the spirit of this collection and label it Y—as in yummy-new-perfume." In a legendary session, it was photographed on Veruschka by Irving Penn in 1965.

being both eye-catching and flawlessly executed.

The simple design also caught the mood of the moment by defining an effortless elegance. Perhaps 1950s' couture clients wanted to enter the room in their Balenciaga gown, secure in the knowledge that "no other women existed," to quote Vreeland; but such thinking began to be dismissed as old-fashioned in the 1960s. The international set had, for example, discovered the luxury ready-to-wear designs of Emilio Pucci, the Italian aristocrat. Pucci's clothes, in his silky proto-psychedelic fabrics, were sensual and relaxing, rather than stiff and formal. And Saint Laurent's infamous antennae picked up on that change, the movement toward clothes that were easy to wear; yet with his innovative skill, and his designs made seamless by apt proportions, choice of fabric, and of color, managed to deliver something different and uniquely stylish—and unexpected—that women longed for. "When a dress of Yves Saint Laurent's appears in a salon or on television, we cry for joy," wrote Marguerite Duras, the French novelist. "For the dress we had never dreamed of is there, and it is just the one we were waiting for, and just that year."

In Saint Laurent's 1966 spring/summer collection, he included a navy pea coat. It was a design first viewed in his premier collection and, in its tailored transformation of the outline of a working man's coat by graceful cutting and fitting of the armholes and attention to the length and fall of the jacket, it would become a classic. However, *Le Smoking* from the following collection would transcend everything. In the style of men's formal eveningwear, Saint Laurent produced an ensemble that had jackets and pants of black wool *grain de poudre* piped with black satin along the pant leg, worn with frilled blouse and black satin ribbon tie. It was a sensation, and the first time that a French male couturier introduced menswear and an androgynous style into his collection. Six months later, he provided the pant suit, further pushing the message. "There is no reason for me to dress women differently from men," he said in 1971. "I don't think a woman is less feminine in pants than a skirt." And in Saint Laurent's designs, with the elegant lines of the jackets, cut to emphasize the femininity of the throat, the waist, and the wrist, and pants tailored so as to lift the behind, they were never masculine.

Indeed, Saint Laurent's idea was that pants gave "a base that would be changeless, for a man and a woman." "It was absolutely a conscious choice," he told *Vogue*'s Joan Juliet Buck. "I've noticed that men were surer of themselves than women, because their clothes don't change—just the color of the shirt and tie—while women were a little abandoned, sometimes terrified, by a fashion that was coming in, or fashion that was only for those under thirty." Nevertheless, Saint Laurent cautioned against a mannish look even if he cited "a photograph of Marlene Dietrich wearing men's clothes" as his chief influence. "A woman dressed as a man must be at the height of her femininity to fight against a costume that isn't hers," he continued. "She should be wonderfully made-up and refined in every detail."

P utting women in pants modernized their closet but, in the late 60s, caused a revolution. Nan Kempner, the American socialite and style icon, was barred from entering a Manhattan restaurant owing to her Yves Saint Laurent pant suit. Not missing a beat, the greyhound-slim Kempner took off her pants and appeared in her tunic, which now became an ultramini dress.

Catherine Deneuve, the French actress who wore Saint Laurent in Buñuel's classic movie *Belle de Jour*, described him as designing for women "with double lives." "His day clothes help a woman confront the world of strangers," she wrote. "They permit her to go everywhere without drawing unwelcome attention and, with their somewhat masculine quality, they give her a certain force." Deneuve also referred to "an immediate sensual experience" when wearing Saint Laurent's couture clothes. "Everything, no matter what it's made of, is always lined in silk satin," she wrote. "That detail is emblematic of his total attitude toward women. He wants to spoil them, to envelop them in the pleasure of his clothes."

Maudie James models two kinds of Rive Gauche suits offering sleek and straight pants with hems that widen. Although Saint Laurent would empower a woman and transform her closet with pants, the idea was initially viewed as scandalous. Photographs by Normal Eales, 1968.

***overleaf** Models Donyale Luna and Moyra Swan wear short couture "barely there dresses" termed as "transparent magic" (left). Popular cover girls, Luna and Swan were ideal to promote Saint Laurent's youthful chic and zest. Luna wears Saint Laurent's strikingly modern "Moonstruck t-shirt" dress (right). Photographs by David Bailey, 1966.*

"HE UNDERSTOOD THAT FASHION HAD TO EXPLORE NEW HORIZONS."

PIERRE BERGÉ

Three examples of Saint Laurent's woven "Hypnotic effects" photographed by David Bailey in 1966. From left, a navy-and-white pullover dress, a cobalt-and-white reefer coat, and a black-and-white suit with square-necked jacket worn by Donyale Luna. When experimenting, Saint Laurent kept to classic and wearable colors.

overleaf *The silk for this art-nouveau-inspired couture dress (left) came from Gustav Zumsteg's Zurich-based Abraham fabrics, recognized for its bold prints and profound influence on Saint Laurent. Photograph by William Klein, 1965. David Bailey's 1967 Vogue cover (right) demonstrated Saint Laurent's vitality and love for vibrant colors, evident on his couture bandanna scarf and gabardine trench coat.*

VOGUE

APRIL 15 1967 4/-

CLOTHES FOR THE ACTION PEOPLE

YOUNG IDEA'S NEW BEAUTY IDEAS
NEW TRICKS, NEW TRENDS, LONDON, PARIS, NEW YORK

FASHION PURE AND SIMPLE
THE MOST DASHING WAY TO LOOK NOW

BEST BUYS
UNDER THE INFLUENCE OF PARIS

"I WAS TORN BETWEEN THE ATTRACTION OF THE PAST AND THE FUTURE THAT URGED ME FORWARD."

YVES SAINT LAURENT

A STYLE REVOLUTION

For Yves Saint Laurent, a couturier who wished that he had invented denim blue jeans, launching Rive Gauche, his ready-to-wear line, made sense in 1966. It also fitted into the 30-year-old's mood. He had become the fashion world's hip young prince and was "sick to death of the couture," and its old-fashioned dictates. "Yves Saint Laurent understood his time," said Pierre Bergé. "He wanted to democratize his metier, which was aristocratic, up to then."

An event in the Ritz Hotel concerning Coco Chanel, the old guard, and Saint Laurent, the new one, illustrated this. He was lunching with Lauren Bacall, the leggy style icon and Hollywood actress, who was sporting a mini skirt. Chanel, who famously hated knees, was appalled. "Saint Laurent, never do short skirts," she croaked. But Chanel had misjudged the formerly shy young man. Saint Laurent had become assertive in his craft and had seriously loosened up in the sixties. Rules and exclusivity in fashion seemed old hat and fusty and he was excited by the new spirit of liberation and equality. For someone who lived a privileged existence and depended upon Bergé, who organized everything in his daily schedule, it was interesting that Saint Laurent was so stirred by the sixties. Putting it down to his acute antennae or sensitive nose that scented change, he told *Vogue*'s Barbara Rose, "I think my success depends on my ability to tune in to the life of the moment, even if I don't really live it."

Saint Laurent Rive Gauche Prêt-à-Porter, the line's official name, was the designer's mission from the beginning. According to Bergé, he resented the "injustice" of the French fashion system that only focused on and favored wealthy women and ignored an entire generation of women who could not afford couture.

At the London opening of his Rive Gauche boutique in 1969, Yves Saint Laurent is flanked by his two muses: Betty Catroux, wearing his iconic "safari" jacket, and Loulou de la Falaise in signature bohemian attire. As predicted by Vogue, his ready-to-wear line proved an immediate success.

overleaf *Saint Laurent embraced the miniskirt and the zeitgeist of the 1960s. Nicole de Lamargé models Saint Laurent's black leather couture suit (left) whose details include black mink edging the short Hussar jacket and a wide hip-level belt. The black patent boots were by shoe designer Roger Vivier, Saint Laurent's close collaborator. Photograph by Brian Duffy, 1966. The actress Catherine Deneuve, photographed in Rive Gauche (right)—a corn-yellow quilted cotton dress with black lace around the hem—by her then husband David Bailey in 1967.*

"Yves formed a new relationship between the fashion creator and the client," said Bergé, suggesting that fashion no longer had to be "an ivory tower existence" concerning those who stayed "at the Ritz." And with the opening of the Rive Gauche boutique, Saint Laurent offered a challenge to the haute couture world and, to quote Bergé again, "became the first ever couturier with a prominent name to create a boutique selling ready-to-wear."

It was a risk. "We had no business plan," recalled Bergé. Yet Rive Gauche, viewed as fashion for the street because of its relatively reasonable prices, was to lead to the full flowering of Saint Laurent's talent as well as empowering him beyond his wildest dreams. *Vogue*'s Gerry Dryansky recalled how, outside of France, "Fashion had burst out into a sort of worldwide citizen's band: everybody's clothes were calling out—proclaiming values, politics, foisting dreams, and invitations." In Paris, Chanel and Balenciaga "turned their backs on all that and died disgusted"; Hubert de Givenchy "kept on dressing his moneyed clients"; whereas André Courrèges "bravely created an original style" between Barbie and Buck Rogers that "reinvented the mood" and lasted for "about two years." However, it became Saint Laurent's hour. His "eclectic, empirical desire to transform the street's own ideas into something similar, better, touched by genius proved the triumphant form of modernism," Dryansky wrote. To quote Marella Agnelli, one of Saint Laurent's famed couture clients, Rive Gauche created "the look" of the times and "fashion took a big step into the future, leaving behind the remote, elitist character it had had in the past."

"Bold, Byronesque," and "dashing" were Vogue's terms for this velvet cape and knickerbocker Rive Gauche suit. Adding a white shirt and a considerable amount of his "gilded chain belts" gave it Saint Laurent's Parisian allure. Photograph by Jeanloup Sieff, 1967.

"It is important for the boutiques to have less expensive clothes so that young women may buy them."

YVES SAINT LAURENT

In Diana Vreeland's estimation, Saint Laurent would have "a fifty-fifty deal with the street." "Half of the time, he is inspired by the street and half of the time, the street gets its style from Yves Saint Laurent," she wrote. "His vehicle to the street is prêt-à-porter—but behind it all are the superb designs of his couture workroom." The couturier would actually keenly separate "church"—haute couture—and "state"—ready-to-wear. "It would be impossible to copy (haute couture) designs in ready-to-wear," he told *Vogue*'s Rose. "No matter how much I might want to at times, the handiwork could not be duplicated by machines. For that reason, I conceive of the prêt-à-porter designs differently in times of machine fabrication." Still, as "The Saint" was quick to emphasize, "there is the same will to perfection" and he gave himself "entirely" to ready-to-wear as he did to couture. His gift for seamlessly shifting between the two worlds also offered another angle to his genius. With his legendary taste and eye that missed nothing, Saint Laurent knew how to create hits for couture—elegant attire that conformed to the racing world and shooting weekends—and hits for ready-to-wear—pieces that suited a café lifestyle and could be worn clutching a boyfriend on the back of his motorbike.

Clara Saint, a beautiful Chilean socialite with international connections, was hired for Rive Gauche's public relations. (A curious aside, but like Saint Laurent's mother, the doll-like Saint was red-haired and green-eyed.) "When Yves decided to create Rive Gauche, he wanted a small out-of-the-way boutique," she recalled. Hence the choice of rue de Tournon, an address in the 6th arrondissement lying on Paris's left bank, the *rive gauche*. "It was young, subversive … [and] had an 'intellectual' connotation," she continued. However, reflecting Saint Laurent's overprotected existence, he presumed that impoverished students from the Sorbonne and other establishments would snap up his clothes, when Rive Gauche would hardly come near Monoprix prices.

Saint Laurent used Abraham's panne velvet fabric, resembling, said Vogue, "liquid mother-of-pearl shadowed with roses in seashell colors," for a long evening dress that is romantic and seductive. Photograph by David Bailey, 1969.

overleaf *Saint Laurent's mastery of color and pattern appeared equally in his couture and ready-to-wear. David Bailey photographs Susan Murray and Maudie James (left) in 1969 in his elaborately constructed long couture gowns in jewel colors of flower pattern and patchwork. Ingrid Boulting adds a flower-child look modeling a Rive Gauche shawl and scarf in a graphic flower print. Photograph by David Bailey, 1970.*

Nevertheless, when Rive Gauche opened its doors on September 26th, there was a stampede. Saint recalled the 1940ft^2/180m^2 boutique being crammed with beauties frantically trying everything on. The appearance of the 23-year-old Catherine Deneuve in a navy blue pea coat made quite an impression on customers queuing down the street. The styles caught the spirit of the youthquake (as Diana Vreeland dubbed the sixties fashion and music revolution) yet added another element: chic. Rive Gauche would further the Parisian's reputation for being chic just as Chanel had, with her little black dress, suit, and bag.

Talking to *Vogue*'s Joan Juliet Buck, Saint Laurent described fashions as being the vitamins of style. "They stimulate, give a healthy jolt … wake you up," he said. And the vim and vigor of his Rive Gauche designs began to spring off the pages of *Vogue*. In the March 1968 issue, the socialite Charlotte Simonin, is photographed around Paris, wearing a series of youthful looks such as a short gray flannel suit, set off by a military collar and kilt-style skirt, and a flouncy black-and-white chintz dress. Parisian in attitude, her long hair and bangs are unkempt while she wears white socks on her long, coltish legs. Six months later, young dynamic Americans such as Tina Barney, Justine Cushing, and the actress Paula Prentiss are photographed in Saint Laurent's wide pants, culottes, and shift dress. Nevertheless, one image eclipses all others, in American *Vogue*'s September issue of 1968. Under the title "Saint Laurent is here!! In New York!!" Diana Ross, caught in Grand Central Station, defines what dazzling means, in flowing tunic top and slithery black chiffon velvet pants, cinched at the waist with a knotted patent leather belt. As if caught in mid-dance, she opens her arms, wide and welcoming. The lead singer of The Supremes, she was black and beautiful, and the spontaneous shot sent an important message: Rive Gauche was for everyone in the United States.

Diana Ross, "the gorgeous star of The Supremes," was also a dedicated follower of fashion. At the New York launch party of Rive Gauche, she radiated charismatic glamour in black chiffon velvet pants and tunic top. Photograph by Jack Robinson, 1968.

Yet another *Vogue* fashion shoot featuring the very blonde model Betty Catroux and the dark-haired singer and actress Jane Birkin unveiled the four-page "Saint Laurent Rive Gauche report." The

jersey pant suit with "long line" tunic, shirtdress, and double-breasted wool coat were effortlessly elegant and fit Dryansky's description of Saint Laurent's clothes as "stockpiles in times of famine."

When Rive Gauche opened in London in 1969, Birkin was photographed for British *Vogue* by Patrick Lichfield, wearing Saint Laurent's white silk ruffled shirt, charcoal and brindled sweater, an ikat-patterned kilt, and a black crushed-velvet suit. "Inimitable looks and individual things," enthused the accompanying text, referring to a range that included "silk scarves dipped in pure paint," "silk tasselled cords," and a palette offering "aubergine, dusky pinks, deep purples, and scarlet." Clare Rendlesham, a former fashion editor, opened the Rive Gauche boutique in Bond Street. "The clothes were amazing: lots of long denim skirts, lace-up safari jackets, long lace-up boots," recalled Jaqumine Bromage, Rendlesham's daughter. The clothes were "advanced and twice as expensive as the other London boutiques like Biba," but gradually women returned, aware that "it was worth paying more for the quality."

Actress and model Jane Birkin enhances Rive Gauche's bohemian allure in a black shirt and wool carpet kilt in a brown and cream stamped patterning —the season's bestseller— that displays classic Saint Laurent style. Photograph by Patrick Lichfield, 1969.

To launch London's Rive Gauche boutique, Saint Laurent showed up in the company of Catroux and Loulou de la Falaise. Cool in sunglasses, Catroux was wearing the iconic safari jacket daringly teamed with thigh-high leather boots, while the smiling de la Falaise, who covered her head with a scarf, chose a denim-style jacket, midi skirt, and suede shoulder pouch. Later described as Saint Laurent's muses, they represented the contrasts of his styles. Catroux played the stark, tomboy role whereas de la Falaise, with her flair for color and accessories, was a sort of flawlessly flamboyant bohemian.

"My success depends on my ability to tune in to the life of the moment ."

YVES SAINT LAURENT

Catroux had met Saint Laurent in 1966. "He picked me up in a night-club," she recalled. "We both had long pale blonde hair, were both very thin, and were both dressed in black leather." Being "sensitive to the same things," they became best friends. The only daughter of Carmen Saint, one of Christian Dior's Brazilian haute couture clients, the chiseled and Nordic-looking Betty had been a house model for Chanel. In 1967, she married interior designer François Catroux, a childhood friend of Saint Laurent. Androgynous and mysterious-looking, Betty was exceptionally bright but preferred to hide her intelligence behind a "I-do-nothing," unambitious façade. Betty was into being young and embracing youth culture and, thanks to her influence, so was Saint Laurent. He questioned whether he really needed to tolerate stuffy couture clients anymore. Surely he was famous enough to cut these ties? Catroux and he would giggle for hours and dance together to the latest pop records. When Saint Laurent had black moods, Betty understood and would commiserate. In spite of her pose, the supposedly *sauvage* Madame Catroux was kind and loyal, which Saint Laurent needed. Women were there to prop him up or adore him just as his mother Lucienne had.

Loulou de la Falaise was also generous and faithful but quite different. Half-English, half-French, she was the daughter of Maxime Birley, the model and society beauty, and Alain, Comte de la Falaise. De la Falaise's childhood had been horrific: after their parent's divorce, she and her younger brother Alexis had been fostered by a series of abusive couples but, unlike Saint Laurent who continually referred to his miserable schooldays and blamed his time in Val-de-Grâce military hospital for his delicate psychological state, de la Falaise kept a stoic silence about her painful past. A woman of substance with a refined taste in fashion, she had been a junior fashion editor at London's *Harper's & Queen*, designed prints for Halston, the fabled American designer, and modeled for American *Vogue*'s Diana Vreeland.

Yves Saint Laurent and Betty Catroux, photographed by Henry Clarke in 1972, having fun in his favorite room, the library, a white room filled with books, 17th-Century Chinese figures, and Lalanne sheep. Both shared a healthy sense of the absurd, while the designer viewed Betty as his physical female equivalent.

***overleaf** Saint Laurent photographed by Bruno Barbey in 1971 surrounded by models from his 1940s-inspired spring/summer show, later referred to as la Collection du Scandale. Though controversial and criticized, the use of fur, exaggerated sophistication, and heightened feminine proportions ended up being extremely influential.*

"SAINT LAURENT CAPTURED THE ZEITGEIST WITH UNCANNY ACUITY."

HAMISH BOWLES

"IT'S TO DO WITH BEING HERE, THE ENERGY AND DYNAMISM OF PARIS."

YVES SAINT LAURENT

Grace Coddington, who styled the shoot, pretends to photograph two models including Louise Despointes; they wear a dyed-red fox bolero, a lime three-quarter length fox jacket, and an emerald-dyed fleecy lamb's wool jacket, from the 40s Collection. "They can wear their furs just as well over evening dress or a skating skirt and perched on high crepe wedges or Allen Jones heels," advised Vogue. Photograph by Duc, 1971.

Saint Laurent had been transfixed by de la Falaise when they first met, through Fernando Sánchez, a classmate from his Chambre Syndicale fashion school. A free spirit, she seemed to sum up spontaneity and yet sophistication, too. Their 1968 courtship began with Saint Laurent sending her a mix of couture clothes and Rive Gauche designs—de la Falaise instinctively knew how to marry styles —and then he offered her a position in his studio which she finally accepted in 1972, joining the more reserved Anne-Marie Muñoz, who ran the studio. Muñoz had met the couturier during his tenure at Christian Dior. Well organized and extremely respectful, her chief aim was to "please Yves." De la Falaise, on the other hand, had her point of view and was prepared to argue with Saint Laurent. He would always admire her honesty and exuberance. "She is a sounding board for my ideas," he told *Vogue*'s Mary Russell. "I bounce thoughts off her and they come back more clear and things begin to happen."

A year before employing her, he invited de la Falaise to his infamous 1971 collection: this had been inspired by Paloma Picasso, whom Saint Laurent recalled seeing at an event "in a turban, platform shoes, one of her mother's 1940s dresses, and outrageously made up." Seated next to Picasso, Loulou had her hair in ringlets and was wearing a bright pink Saint Laurent satin jacket and purple shorts. They were put in the audience, in order to talk about the show afterward and demonstrate support. Clearly, Saint Laurent was nervous about the collection: it was different from his other couture shows and nothing like anything else in fashion, at that time. After a lineup of 1940s-style dresses with plunging necklines, seen under fur chubbies (short, chunky fur coats) in green and blue, were designs like a velvet coat covered in lipstick kisses, large velvet turbans, puffed sleeves, ruched waists, and wedge heels. The louche styling of the models appeared shocking. Their lips were smeared with lipstick and it was evident that none was wearing underwear, particularly a voluptuous model whose large breasts bounced freely under her red dress.

Saint Laurent explored the color and sensual potential of knits as thoroughly as with other materials. Described as "patched, flowered, striped, and plaid," a signature Rive Gauche mood is captured by a printed silk shirt, belted tank top, and printed skirt. Photograph by Barry Lategan, 1971.

Vogue's enthusiasm for Rive Gauche continued throughout the 1970s: "Take home more Saint Laurent looks—like his dressed up shorts ... Adore his new classic cardigans and pleats." Photograph by Peter Knapp, 1972.

overleaf *Charlotte Rampling, another British model-turned-actress, suited Saint Laurent's effortless elegance (left). Here, she wears his couture cardigan, which Vogue, despite its glamour, called "a poem of understatement," a glittering top, and navy blue skirt. Photograph by David Bailey, 1972. A chef d'oeuvre, the black-satin detailed Le Smoking (right) was easy to dress up – with fur, for example – or down. Photograph by Peter Knapp, 1971.*

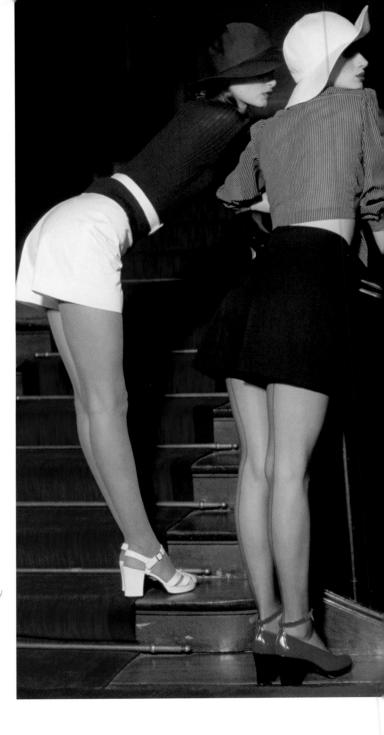

Eugenia Sheppard denounced the experience as "completely hideous." Nor did any of the French audience approve. It was generally felt that referencing the 1940s brought up shameful memories of France under the Occupation.

Eighteen months later, Saint Laurent told *Vogue*'s Mary Russell that the collection, which had proved successful and influential, was his reaction to the fashion landscape: "The gypsies, all those long skirt and bangles on middle-aged women in town—in the middle of the twentieth century!" He claimed that it was "a humorous protest" except it was taken seriously. "People thought it wasn't 'Me' but it was; they don't know about my reactions. I am quiet but inside there is an explosion."

Saint Laurent's "explosion" was apparent when he launched his first male fragrance in 1971 and used his own naked self in the advertising campaign. "He wanted to create a scandal," said Jeanloup Sieff who took the black-and-white portrait. Indeed, the controversial image was Saint Laurent's idea not Sieff's. Justly proud of his trim and taut physique, there was also a Christlike look about Saint Laurent who then had midlength hair and a beard. Did he view himself as fashion's savior? Many women thought he was.

In the early 1970s, there was a sense that Saint Laurent had arrived at a relatively tranquil and confident moment in his life. "After more than ten years as a designer, I now know exactly what to do. I cannot deviate from my style," he told *Vogue*'s Russell. "I have made my experiments and mistakes. Now I am sure. Style consists of very little. You don't go too far to the left or too far to the right."

In his heyday, the main secret behind Saint Laurent's style was that everything he designed seemed alluring and apt. Nicknamed *le maître* (master) by Parisians, it was because they could rely on his designs, whatever the occasion. Empowered by his faultless proportions, bold color sense, and use of sensual fabrics, women felt feminine and seductive. During the day, it might be structured pant

Jeanloup Sieff's portrait of Yves Saint Laurent, used to advertise the designer's YSL aftershave in 1971, was groundbreaking on several fronts. It was the first time in fashion history that a fragrance maker had posed for his own advertising campaign, and Saint Laurent opted to do so in the nude.

suits softened by a satin blouse with pussycat bow or dresses that subtly enhanced the figure. At night, he either created little black dresses or *Le Smoking*-type suits that glowed with glamour, or wildly embellished pieces that dominated by dazzling.

Many friends put his confidence and tranquility down to his discovering Marrakech and buying a house there in 1967. Called Dar El Hanch—meaning house of the serpent—it was in the ancient medina. "Here he spends three months of every year," enthused *Vogue*. "December and June when he prepares his collections, and August, when he relaxes." Invisible from the street behind its heavy, nail-studded door and thick walls, the house inside was secluded and enchanting. It meandered up and down whitewashed staircases, around a shady inner courtyard with a fountain, out onto vine-wreathed balconies, and up to a flat roof overlooking the palm-fringed city.

There were elements of Marrakech that reminded him of his childhood in Oran: this was perfect for an individual obsessed with nostalgia and the novels of Marcel Proust. There was also a romance to the place that appealed to his aesthetic sense. "On each street corner in Marrakech, you encounter groups that are impressive in their intensity," he told Laurence Benaïm, his original biographer. "Men and women, where pink, blue, green, and violet caftans mingle. These groups look as if they have been drawn and painted … by Delacroix." To quote Betty Catroux during that period, "Paris is the mirror of anxieties. Marrakech is the place where he is happy."

This exotic shoot by Duc in 1976 captures Marrakech's influence on Rive Gauche's collection, described by Vogue as having "wrapped knotted heads, harem pants, belts of vivid silk thread." Naturally, Saint Laurent's accessories were luxurious and included metallic gold turbans, and ivory bead necklaces.

"Oran as a child during the war marked me … in Marrakech I found the climate of my childhood."

YVES SAINT LAURENT

"ALL CREATIVE WORK IS PAINFUL
AND FASHION IS VERY, VERY DIFFICULT.
IT PLAYS ON ALL MY ANXIETIES."

YVES SAINT LAURENT

THE HOUSE THAT YVES
AND PIERRE BUILT

The 1970s evolved into the glory decade for Yves Saint Laurent. Women exuded sensuality in his clothes, as exemplified by two portraits in British *Vogue*. Catherine Deneuve is stretched out on the designer's couch, wearing a gray pinstripe gabardine pant suit and strict silk blouse, whereas Bianca Jagger, the rock star's wife, is spread across her bed at the mythic left bank L'Hôtel, wearing a long fuchsia pink chiffon dress, black hose, and diamanté peep-toe sandals.

That Saint Laurent could produce so perfectly such contrasting styles, the disciplined and the indulgent, explained why key fashion editors and important retailers hungered for Saint Laurent's couture and ready-to-wear shows, viewing them as the main event.

The graceful Bianca Jagger and Saint Laurent had a special affinity, eternally marked by the unforgettable white Saint Laurent couture suit she wore to her wedding. Here she is photographed in Paris by Eric Boman in 1974 wearing a long chiffon and elastic cocktail dress.

"If my clothes are right, and I believe they are," he told Joan Juliet Buck, "it is because I think I understand what women want." Adding to his triumphs was the success of his Rive Gauche Pour Homme line, which the designer had originally started because he could not find clothes for himself. Two years later, it boasted eclectic clients like actor Helmut Berger, ballet dancer Rudolf Nureyev, and playwright Harold Pinter. Further fame came from the fabled Saint Laurent lifestyle that he officially shared with Pierre Bergé and consisted of homes in Paris, New York, Manhattan, Marrakech, and a chateau in Normandy.

There was also the personal charisma of Saint Laurent, who had acquired iconic status, unusual for a fashion designer. He had become as famous as Andy Warhol and Mick Jagger. *L'Amour Fou*, the Saint Laurent documentary, unveils a short black-and-white home movie that shows these three individuals in each other's company. Filmed at the designer's apartment in the rue de Babylone, noted for its Jean-Michel Frank interiors, a longhaired Jagger in tracksuit is hunched over the Ruhlmann piano, tinkling at the keys. Warhol in blazer and jeans, seated on an armchair, opts to smile but remain mute. It is very much Saint Laurent's moment. Wearing a suit and bow tie, he smiles and camps it up for the camera, enthusing about his series of mini Warhol portraits.

"YVES SAINT LAURENT IS ALL ABOUT EXPRESSION. SOME DESIGNERS DO CLOTHING THAT IS MERELY COLOR AND SHAPE, HIS ALWAYS SAYS SOMETHING."

CATHERINE DENEUVE

Exemplifying the "fire-behind-the-ice" Parisian bourgeois beauty that inspired the couturier, Catherine Deneuve was always a stalwart "Yves" friend and client. Here she sports a couture gabardine pinstripe pant suit with caramel silk shirt. Photographed in Saint Laurent's apartment by Oliviero Toscani in 1976.

Saint Laurent was having a second lease of life, fueled by his roaring career and a lack of inhibition via his discovery of casual sex, recreational drugs, and hard alcohol. One of the designer's chief complaints was that he had missed out on his youth owing to early fame and his responsibilities at Christian Dior. However, because of the atmosphere of Paris in the 1970s—a sizzling and decadent period—Saint Laurent found the excuse to self-indulge on a monumental scale. Being compulsive, he tended to go too far, though instinctively he knew that Bergé was ready and waiting to save him. Whatever the situation—even if Saint Laurent crashed his car because of a lover's tiff with a toy boy—he could rely on the highly competent Bergé to sort it out. In the drama, passion, and dynamics of their liaison, which affected and occasionally emotionally drained their immediate circle, the Saint Laurent-Bergé relationship was a textbook example of the addict and the enabler.

Whatever the occasion, women confidently depended upon Saint Laurent's Rive Gauche in the 1970s. Under Vogue's *title, "Are you huntin', shootin', fishin' clothes?" Norman Parkinson photographed this suggested outfit in 1973, the cloak, jacket, and skirt in traditional loden, soft suede, and tweed.*

Still, the brilliant Bergé convinced himself otherwise. "What endures in Yves is his sense of childhood, and his refusal to leave it," he said. "His work absorbed him and he took refuge in a cocoon—imaginary or otherwise—which he created totally and which he inhabited full time. Yves is [the poets] Hölderlin and Rimbaud. A fire maker." Had Bergé disappeared, Saint Laurent might have been forced to shape up and change. Yet his business partner did not abandon him, both smitten by his genius and aware that their growing empire depended on looking after Saint Laurent's talent. Besides, his partner was not the only one behaving badly in Paris.

For an article entitled "70s Paris, The Party Years," Karl Lagerfeld, at the time Chloé's ready-to-wear designer, told *W* magazine that he "hated to be out of town for more than 24 hours … There was the feeling that, wherever you were in Europe, you did whatever you had to do to make it back to Paris for drinks at the Café de Flore, then dinner and dancing at Le Sept." But apart from the actress and model Marisa Berenson, who lived on orange juice and meditation, and Lagerfeld himself, who never dabbled in drugs or alcohol, fashionable Paris had become as decadent as Manhattan in the Jazz Age or Berlin in the 1930s, with vodka the drink and cocaine the drug of choice. Berenson, the star of the movie *Cabaret*, recalled "a complete intensity about everything" and how "it was a dangerous time for some … Like anything that doesn't have boundaries, many people went too far." Nevertheless, there was an amazing exuberance and euphoria and a sense that something different and brand new was happening in Paris, a sort of unofficial creative movement, featuring fashion talents such as Saint Laurent, Lagerfeld, the designer Kenzo Takada, and the illustrator Antonio Lopez, Loulou de la Falaise, and *Vogue* photographers like Helmut Newton and Guy Bourdin.

The Austrian actor Helmut Berger was the perfect poster-boy for Saint Laurent's Rive Gauche Pour Homme; he and the designer were physically similar and equally ambiguously seductive. Here, Berger wears an evening tunic, satin pants, and belt with metal butterfly buckle. Photograph by David Bailey, 1971.

According to Marian McEvoy, then working at *Woman's Wear Daily*, it was a time "of such extravagance" in Paris. "No one had discreet little cars or passe-partout suits. There was no slinking in wearing a simple black dress—people were there to show off." "We would just throw together some kind of turban or experiment with something ethnic," said de la Falaise. "The idea was, 'what can I invent tonight?'" It was a kind of inventiveness that blurred the distinction between day and night. "Private life, professional life, fashion business, and fashion expression —it all overlapped," said Lagerfeld. Later, Saint Laurent described all the feverish partying as boosting his creativity. "We went out constantly but we also worked so much," he told *W* magazine. "Going out only made us more creative."

"Even if I am doing a man's suit, I try to make it feminine."

YVES SAINT LAURENT

"DRESSING IS A WAY OF LIFE."

YVES SAINT LAURENT

"Are you visibly Saint Laurent?" asked Vogue *of these "wicked black chiffons, shrugged off the shoulders" photographed by Guy Bourdin in 1977, styled by Grace Coddington using models Kathy Quirk, Audrey Matson, and Carrie Nygren. Every item was signature Rive Gauche, ranging from the feathered chiffon, gilt, and silk braid accessories to the iconic black satin, gold lace shoes.*

Vogue's André Leon Talley recalled a night out on the town with Saint Laurent and Betty Catroux. "Dressed to the nines for a night at Le Sept club, we would start at his apartment on rue de Babylone. First we might sit in his grand salon, with a Goya perched on an artist's easel surrounded by Picassos mounted on the walls and museum quality Art Deco furniture. Downstairs in the white library, we fueled ourselves with caviar and chilled Stolichnaya like runners before a marathon." Occasionally, Saint Laurent's absent-minded behavior needed to be watched. One of his "ubiquitous dangling cigarettes" caused a fire on the white couch that Catroux and Leon Talley quickly doused "with water from the ice bucket."

"Organize yourself ... sepia," said Vogue recommending the pale and reddish-brown hues of Saint Laurent's cloche hat, the silk bow around the neck, and fox fur around the collar for the Rive Gauche woman. Photograph by Barry Lategan, 1974.

During that period, Leon Talley described Saint Laurent as speaking "like a shy schoolchild, startled at being called upon to talk." "But in top form, and in private, he was wickedly witty and funny: his imitations of competitors were nothing less than mini theatrical productions," he wrote. When staying at Château Gabriel, the Normandy retreat where Bergé would deposit guests by helicopter, and was decorated by interior designer Jacques Grange, Leon Talley was tickled by how every guest room was named after a character from Proust's *A la Recherche du Temps Perdu*. "Most of the time, we would sit in the winter garden, full of exotic hothouse plants and palm trees, watching him spoil Moujik [he gave every dog he ever had the same name, which means "Russian peasant" in French] by slipping him salami from the hors d'oeuvres tray."

"I belong to a world devoted to elegance."

YVES SAINT LAURENT

"A MODERN SUIT,
A BEAUTIFUL BODY
LIKE A PERFECT
AIRPLANE."

JOAN JULIET BUCK

*Seventies superstars: illustrator
Antonio Lopez play-acting with
model Jerry Hall, styled by Grace
Coddington and photographed
by Norman Parkinson in 1975.
Vogue said that "the scene here
is pure Saint Laurent," and it
was. The looks of both Hall and
Lopez—ranging from shirts,
white cotton pants, and trench
coat—were entirely Rive Gauche.*

At Le Sept, Saint Laurent would sit in a corner, usually next to Catroux and stare: being curious, he was constantly searching out and intrigued by different ideas and moods. After all, Paloma Picasso's 1940s dress had inspired his most notorious collection in 1971. When talking to *Vogue*'s Mary Russell in 1972, Saint Laurent admitted that he was "always looking … My eyes never stop." Regarding his work, he mentioned "a new appreciation for the almost lost art of the artisans, the ones who could not exist without couture," and cited the importance of his collaboration with the Swiss-based Gustav Zumsteg who ran the legendary Abraham fabrics. "We feel the same currents and trends at the same time —he, way off in Zurich, me here in Paris. Geography has nothing to do with talent," he said. "Once, when we met after several months' separation to discuss ideas, I talked about a fabric I saw in my mind—an idea for a dress—and he pulled the fabric right out of his pocket."

Zumsteg would be on hand for Saint Laurent's Opéra Les Ballets Russes couture collection in July 1976, which *Vogue* entitled, "The Romance that shook the World." To the sound of Verdi and other opera music, his models appeared in a sumptuous mix of velvet vests trimmed with sable, full skirts, and blouses in rich, exotic colors, gold lamé boots, and bejeweled headdresses; bosoms swelled, and waists were corseted. It was an intensely sensual performance, and it resulted in a wildly emotional standing ovation from the audience.

Camaraderie and style, exemplified by actress-model Anjelica Huston, shoe designer Manolo Blahnik and model Grace Coddington; styled by Coddington and photographed in Sardinia by their friend David Bailey in 1974. Huston is wearing Saint Laurent: Rive Gauche's bone-buttoned wool cape, pleat skirt, cardigan, muslin blouse, and court shoes.

overleaf *The curvaceous Swedish model Carrie Nygren gives a sexual charge to Saint Laurent's designs in an "all-out glamour to outshine anything" shoot for* Vogue *by Lothar Schmid in 1976. On the left, she wears Rive Gauche's black mousseline and gold lamé flowered top and black-and-gold lamé skirt; for the cover, right, Rive Gauche's red lamé blouse, golden braid choker, and bauble earrings.*

"Classics are something you can wear all your life. I do classic things for women to have the same assurance with their clothes that men have with theirs."

YVES SAINT LAURENT

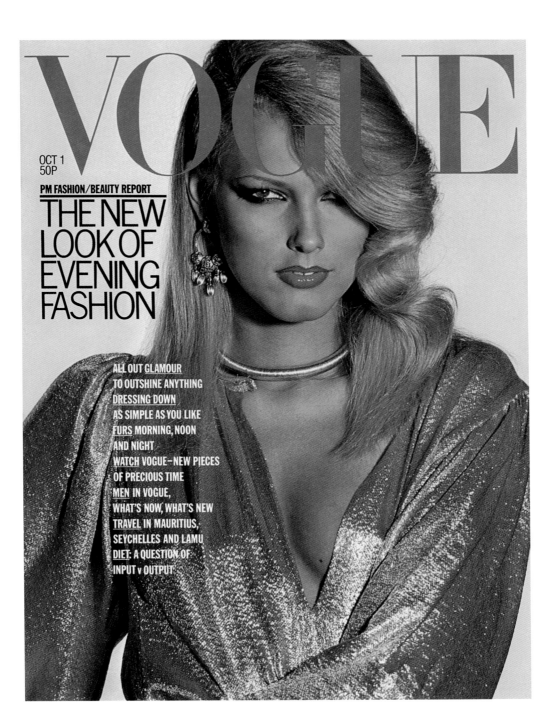

VOGUE

OCT 1
50P

PM FASHION/BEAUTY REPORT

THE NEW LOOK OF EVENING FASHION

ALL OUT GLAMOUR
TO OUTSHINE ANYTHING
DRESSING DOWN
AS SIMPLE AS YOU LIKE
FURS MORNING, NOON
AND NIGHT
WATCH VOGUE—NEW PIECES
OF PRECIOUS TIME
MEN IN VOGUE,
WHAT'S NOW, WHAT'S NEW
TRAVEL IN MAURITIUS,
SEYCHELLES AND LAMU
DIET: A QUESTION OF
INPUT v OUTPUT

"Just a ruffle off the shoulders" is how Vogue described Rive Gauche's Liberty-printed chiffon worn by Marie Helvin and photographed by her husband David Bailey in 1975.

overleaf *The exuberance of Saint Laurent's Opéra Les Ballets Russes couture collection triumphed particularly in the US, even influencing the high street. Vogue described it as "small-waisted, big skirted," firing "memory and desire" and defining "high romance." On the left, embellished chiffon, a turban, and velvet bodice; on the right, Kirat Young models a silk quilted jacket and billowing skirt. Photographs by Duane Michals, 1976.*

In *Vogue*, Duane Michals' four-page fashion shoot illustrated the collection, featuring "glorious heroines" in designs in which "no scale of evening is unaccounted for, the luxe and width of skirt" yet managed to raise "the curtain on a new area of day-into-easy evening dressing." When questioned by British *Vogue*'s Leslie White about the collection, Saint Laurent claimed, "Paris was really in the doldrums at the time, people were saying that this city was finished. So I decided to make one of the richest, most extraordinary collections of my career."

In fact, it was Saint Laurent who was in "the doldrums." He had suffered a nervous collapse that was treated by the American Hospital in Neuilly as severe depression. His fragile state was the result of Bergé walking out. Packing his suitcase, Bergé had left their rue de Babylone apartment and moved to the Hôtel Lutetia. After giving endless warnings to Saint Laurent about his intolerable behavior, Bergé had made the domestic break, even if he remained permanently in the wings for the designer.

Nevertheless, the suffering caused by Bergé's departure —his rock had abandoned him—had produced "a violent explosion of fantasy." It illustrated Saint Laurent's favorite line from Proust: "In his suffering, he found the ability to create." Viewing the task as a personal and dreamlike assignment, he decided to include everything that he admired in life, so not only did the collection have the colorful and exotic flamboyance of the Ballets Russes, but also the quiet richness of works of art he loved, like Vermeer's portrait of *Girl with a Pearl Earring*. "I have always wanted to do a collection that was a reflection of my taste," he said. The American retailers reveled in the lushness of fabric and embroidery—American women were going through an exuberant phase; the French purists did not. Although the details were exquisite, some felt it old-fashioned, conservative, and cumbersome. "These are not clothes for women who take the Métro," the designer confessed. Indeed, in price and tone, they suited the chauffeur-driven superrich.

Six months later, Saint Laurent was back at the American Hospital. In spite of this, in three weeks, he designed the Carmen collection —from his bed. It was highly dramatic, the main theme centering on black velvet corselet bodices teamed with taffeta skirts. It had been influenced by a scandalous production of *Carmen*, directed by Roland Petit in 1950, starring Zizi Jeanmaire. "I have an enormous tenderness for Roland and Zizi, they really marked my youth artistically," he told *Vogue*'s Joan Juliet Buck. In their "News Report," *Vogue* exclaimed, "Women loved it and the men went nuts about it." It was sultry and easy to wear, and its appeal was intensified by a proliferation of jet earrings and chokers. "It was a personal explosion," Saint Laurent said after the show, which began with the singer Grace Jones, counted 281 outfits and lasted a staggering two and half hours. Backstage, the couturier was described by *Women's Wear Daily* as "pale and weak" as well as "brushing tears from his face" as he greeted admirers. He was then rushed back to hospital.

There would be more of the same psychological problems for the next two years, yet Saint Laurent continued to triumph with colorful couture collections like Opium and Broadway which electrified his clients. In the 1977 December issue, Diana Vreeland was quoted by British *Vogue* as saying: "Yves Saint Laurent has wandered through history with a sort of extraordinary butterfly net and he's caught some of the most beautiful attributes of women from all ages." None of the collections were his innovative best but they demonstrated his fertile, imaginative mind. "I don't try to make a revolution in my clothes each time, I don't try to be sensational," he told *Vogue*'s Polly Devlin. "But I think it's normal to have something new because life is renewing all the time, and I'm not fixed or static in my thinking or emotions or my designing."

Owing to Bergé's business acumen, their company was free of outside ownership in 1972. "I told him it would take ten years for us to become profitable," Bergé told *Vogue*'s Gerry Dryansky, "and I was right, to the year." Following the business plan of Christian Dior, Bergé "began to capitalize in earnest" on the Saint Laurent name. This reached a peak of success in 1974 when Maurice Bidermann, who made and distributed Pierre Cardin menswear in America, stopped working with Cardin and chose Yves Saint Laurent instead and, according to Dryansky, "immediately sold $50 million worth, wholesale, of Saint Laurent blazers and suits that year." At the end of the 1970s, the Saint Laurent Empire counted over one hundred Rive Gauche ready-to-wear boutiques and a large array of Saint Laurent licensed products bringing in annual net royalties of $18 million.

overleaf Saint Laurent's Carmen collection epitomized a dramatic dressiness, apt for the period, and inspired a Vogue shoot —"The Lady is a Vamp"—and cover, photographed by Willie Christie in 1977. On the left, Marcie James models Rive Gauche's cotton bodice with bow and poppy in her hair; on the right, Rive Gauche's flamenco flair includes chiffon blouses, flouncy skirts, silk-fringed shawl, and tassel earclips.

In May 1977 Loulou de la Falaise married Thadée Klossowski, the painter Balthus's charming and good-looking son. A few months later, Saint Laurent and Bergé gave them a wedding ball for 500 guests at the Châlet des Iles, set in the swan-filled lagoon of the Bois de Boulogne, which required gondolas to reach it. Demonstrating Saint Laurent's particular fondness for de la Falaise, he had envisioned and made the entire green-and-white decor, from the awning-striped tent to the enormous columns crossed with satin. Just as they were nearing the end of the decoration, they realized that Saint Laurent had not designed her gown. There was a mild panic in the *flou* ateliers (dressmaking studios) to create the midnight-blue chiffon dress shot with gold, designed to resemble a summer's night sky in Marrakech, which had to be kept together by uncomfortable elastic between Loulou's stick-thin thighs. The morning of the party, she had made the diamanté moon and star headpiece herself, using cardboard, glitter, and glue.

"Things have been wonderful since Loulou came. It is important to have her beside me when I'm working on a collection … I trust her reactions."

YVES SAINT LAURENT

VOGUE

MAR1
60p

the best of everywhere ®

international
fashion & beauty

who's
who

and
who
are
you?

(however
you see yourself
there's a look
that's right
for you now)

**insider's guide
to Paris**

**new techniques
in name dropping**

**is pain
good for you?**

"I CANNOT WORK WITHOUT THE MOVEMENT OF THE HUMAN BODY.

YVES SAINT LAURENT

At this most glamorous of parties, Saint Laurent wearing a dinner jacket, a red cummerbund, and tennis shoes was in gregarious form, chatting and dancing with friends. The next morning, an alarming amount of syringes were found, implying heroin use. In certain circles, the lethal drug had replaced cocaine.

With the opening of Le Palace nightclub in March 1978—Le Sept-owner Fabrice Emaer's idea of a cooler and less sanitized Studio 54—it was obvious that a darker dissoluteness had crept in. "On one side, it was about going to parties and looking great, but the other side was pretty heavy—doing every drug in sight," said Marisa Berenson. To inaugurate the much-awaited event—Le Palace would become *the* nightspot in the late 1970s—Emaer had chosen Grace Jones to perform. She opened with "La Vie en Rose." Saint Laurent, however, disapproved of Jones's choice of headdress. Without a word and indicating his accepted authority, he simply went behind her and wrapped the singer's head in his scarf.

In the dependable chic of Rive Gauche's classics, Saki Reed Burton illustrates "great black looks with white," modeling a black velvet dirndl, loose boxy jacket with double ruffle Pierrot collar, and similarly ruffled white silk shirt. Photograph by Eric Boman, 1977.

previous page *Arja Töyrylä flaunts the Matisselike colors of the Carmen collection. In smock blouse, striped wool harem pants, braided jacket, and fez, Vogue says she is "jumping with joie de vivre as Saint Laurent's Francoturk." Photograph by Willie Christie, 1977.*

overleaf *François Lamy photographed "Paris with a dash of style" for Vogue in 1979: on the left, Mira Tibblin models Rive Gauche's "heavenly" loose wool pant suit, perked up by polka-dot shirt and lacquered straw pillbox; on the right, Karen Howard wears a sweater, straight skirt, satin scarf, and lacquered straw hat in Rive Gauche's luscious colors. laboressita dio et.*

Several months later, there was the New York launch of Opium, Saint Laurent's bestselling fragrance, whose heady scent defined the era. Helmut Newton photographed the advertising campaign at Saint Laurent's house in his mirrored Buddha room. Choosing Jerry Hall was an inspired idea. It was at the height of her modeling career and, having posed for endless *Vogue* covers, she knew exactly how to smolder and provoke. Above her mass of curled blond hair, there was a line that read *Opium, pour celles qui s'adonnent à Yves Saint Laurent* that, depending on the translation, could either mean "for those who abandon themselves" or "for those who are addicted to Saint Laurent." The overtones of drug addiction typified Opium's risqué reputation. When launched in Europe in the fall of 1977, the fragrance had been a hit, particularly at Christmas time.

"I LOVE GOLD, A MAGICAL COLOR, FOR THE REFLECTION OF A WOMAN. IT IS THE COLOR OF THE SUN."

YVES SAINT LAURENT

OPIUM,
pour celles qui s'adonnent à Yves Saint Laurent.

Parfums
Yves Saint Laurent

In America, however, Opium's name caused an outcry with a group of Chinese Americans. They demanded a change of name and public apology from Saint Laurent, insisting that the drug was a holocaustlike reminder of abuse and bloodshed in their country's history. Oddly enough, the controversy worked in Opium's favor; it ignited interest and soaring sales.

Squibb, the owners of the YSL perfume division, agreed to spend $250,000 on Opium's American launch party. Organized by Marina Schiano, the vice-president of YSL in America, the event was held on "The Peking," a magnificent barque with four masts. Eight hundred invitations had been sent out. Guests were greeted by an extravagant arrangement of 5,000 cattleya orchids, a Proustian reference for Saint Laurent's benefit, as well as a 1,000-pound (450 kg) bronze Buddha statue that had been hoisted on board. *Women's Wear Daily* had written a sour article implying that the soirée was a failure, in spite of the presence of Saint Laurent, de la Falaise, and his top American couture clients. But it is possible that *WWD's* owner John Fairchild—fashion's mischief-maker—had fallen out with Bergé and was causing trouble. This was the first time that a party with an A-list cast had been organized to sell and promote, rather than just celebrate. It marked a changing tide in the beauty world. And it was a tide that was about to hit fashion.

"Yves Saint Laurent invents a reality and adds it to the other, the one he has not made. And he fuses all of this in a paradoxical harmony—often revolutionary, always dazzling."

MARGUERITE DURAS

"A DRESS IS NOT STATIC, IT HAS A RHYTHM."

YVES SAINT LAURENT

"I AM NO LONGER CONCERNED WITH
SENSATION AND INNOVATION BUT
WITH THE PERFECTION OF MY STYLE."

YVES SAINT LAURENT

A GIANT OF COUTURE

On December 5, 1983, Yves Saint Laurent's retrospective opened at the Metropolitan Museum of Art. Held at the Museum's Costume Institute and showcasing twenty-five years of his work, it was an incredible compliment since it was the first time that they had ever devoted an exhibition to a living designer. "Why Yves Saint Laurent?" wrote Diana Vreeland who had curated the exhibition. "Because he is a genius, because he knows everything about women." Vreeland, who had been at the Costume Institute since 1972, then continued, "The reason I selected Yves is that for twenty-six years he has kept women's clothes on the same high level. He is followed across the oceans of the world by women who look young, live young, and are young no matter what their age."

The exhibition was a hit and boasted a million visitors. It consisted of 243 pieces and showed a tremendous amount of his collections from the late 1970s and early 1980s. The range of suits and dresses were all faultlessly constructed and conjured up the elaborate requirements of that time, yet they now look a little dated. In the exhibition, Saint Laurent was quoted as saying, "Luxury is above all an attitude of the heart. I never considered it as something that revolves around money, jewels, or furs." Nevertheless, looking at the catalog's outfits, which were often spectacular showstoppers—i.e. once worn, never forgotten but difficult to wear again—there is a nagging sense that only the seriously wealthy could afford the dresses. Whereas Saint Laurent's black cocktail dresses for Dior were absolutely timeless and still seem contemporary, as do all his iconic classics from the 1960s: his gray satin tunic worn with velvet skirt, his pea coat, or *caban* of navy-blue wool twill with gold buttons, his safari jacket, and his *Smokings*. There are also his simple yet modern looks from the early 1970s: a beige jacket worn with black *grain de poudre* wool pants, a midcalf length black crepe and velvet dress, a black wool gabardine jumpsuit, and a long silk crepe evening shirtdress with matching scarf.

Talisa Soto is photographed by Bruce Weber for Vogue's *"The New Vamps" in 1982. her stretched limbs and toned body, typical of the new generation of models, show to perfection Saint Laurent's couture black Moreau velvet and ruby Perceval satin gown.*

overleaf Christy Turlington photographed by Patrick Demarchelier for Vogue's *"What Really Counts from The International Collections" story and cover in 1987. Here, Rive Gauche's quilted reversible satin jacket, silk cloqué shirt, and short skirt offer luminous color and instant appeal.*

VOGUE

JULY
£2·00

fashion's key points

WHAT REALLY
COUNTS FROM
THE INTERNATIONAL
COLLECTIONS

SCANDALOUS
BEHAVIOUR

POLITICAL WIVES

WOMEN
DESIGNERS

seasonless dressing—

CLOTHES FOR
THE REAL LIFE

The late 1970s and early 1980s work was superbly executed, yet it was evident that Yves Saint Laurent had changed. He had moved on from having his finger on the pulse and being innovative, and had turned to dressing the middle-aged and established. During an interview with *Vogue*'s Barbara Rose in 1978, he claimed to be disappointed with the younger generation, describing them as lacking a "message to transmit." Five years later, he took it further with Joan Juliet Buck. "Today's look is very destructive for the kids themselves who are denying their own beauty," he said. "I'm aware of a desire to ruin and distort harmony, and it's worrying. It's purely gratuitous, but it can go very far, and it seems to create a sort of sect without values. So I feel isolated from these kids."

Saint Laurent was only 47 years old yet he was complaining like Chanel, in her later years. He had turned into the sort of person whom he would have avoided during his youth. Still, it has to be stressed that the 1980s were an unhappy decade for Saint Laurent, unhappiness compounded by the public and inaccurate rumors that he had AIDS. Of course there were accolades such as the Metropolitan's retrospective, but his hedonistic behavior in the 1970s had caught up with him. A haze of serious drugs, powerful tranquilizers, and alcohol had taken a toll on his health and his mood. Isolated and unhappy, he occasionally turned into a hermit who had lost his joie de vivre. Naturally, his friends like Betty Catroux rallied around him, and Anne-Marie Muñoz and Loulou de la Falaise supported him by running his studio, but Saint Laurent was often inebriated, slurring his words, and making little sense. Old friends like Victoire, the former Dior model, were shocked by his frazzled state and self-destructive behavior. Perhaps unsurprisingly, Saint Laurent had to be saved from an alcohol-induced coma in 1985.

Suzanne Lanza photographed by Neil Kirk in 1989 softens the strict lines of Saint Laurent's "timelessly appropriate" Rive Gauche hip-length wool jacket and short cream wool straight skirt.

"It's a perfection of line. It's a perfection of material."

YVES SAINT LAURENT

Meanwhile, the image-conscious Pierre Bergé hid as much of this as he could from the media. From the 1980s he had one aim: to get Saint Laurent's designs into museums and mark him as the most important couturier of the second half of the twentieth century. The Metropolitan retrospective certainly realized this goal, since it toured for a staggering seven years and traveled to Bejing, Paris, Moscow, St. Petersburg, Sydney, and Tokyo. Being Saint Laurent's most fervent supporter, Bergé must have privately realized that the couturier's best designing years were behind him. Yet, instead of letting the cracks show, Bergé built up Saint Laurent's reputation by reminding the public of his extraordinary body of work. It was an inspired, effective idea and also a rightful claim. The exhibitions and numerous anniversary celebrations demonstrated that there was nothing that Saint Laurent had not done.

Nevertheless, Bergé was marketing his Yves as the untouchable, the rightful heir of Coco Chanel. This was to change when the house of Chanel announced the appointment of Karl Lagerfeld on September 15, 1982. Lagerfeld, who had been a runner-up to Saint Laurent in the 1954 International Wool Secretariat, who had been a friend of Saint Laurent during his years at Dior, but who then had fallen out with Saint Laurent and Bergé in 1970s over Jacques de Bascher, Lagerfeld's aristocratic and highly desired boyfriend. Somewhat typically, the house of Saint Laurent took the news badly, particularly the designer himself, who had always felt such infinity with Chanel; she, like him, had been influenced by androgyny, highlighted the appeal of black and placed style over fashion. "Chanel found perfection and stayed with it," he told Dryansky. Certain members of Saint Laurent's camp even presumed that Lagerfeld had taken on Chanel to hurt their Yves. Laughable as this claim sounds, it did betray the house of Saint Laurent's unrealistic sense that no other designer mattered apart from *Yves le Maître*.

"Elegance Grise," said Vogue of Saint Laurent's unbeatable Rive Gauche classic of a gray wool-flannel suit with wrap around skirt, given Parisian poise by model Laetitia Firmin-Didot. Photograph by Eamonn J McCabe, 1989.

overleaf *Saint Laurent would always continue to do sumptuous and magical evening dresses, like this Hurel tulle couture gown with tight bodice and sashed waist (left), photographed in 1981 at the Crillon Hotel by John Stember. "Très Belle Époque," said Vogue of Saint Laurent's couture pairing of a Taroni satin dolman-sleeved cape and a Moreau velvet strapless dress (right) photographed on Marie Lindfors by Terence Donovan in 1983.*

After a few shaky seasons, the Chanel collections of the ever-industrious Lagerfeld became seriously successful. Being accessible, amusing, and quotable in four languages, Lagerfeld was viewed as a journalist's dream, and a parade of admiring articles began. Saint Laurent, on the other hand, remained his reticent self. As a result, Saint Laurent's press department pushed the charms of Loulou de la Falaise—a winner with the media since she looked chic in every outfit, was photogenic, and was articulate about the designer's work. For their September 1987 issue, British *Vogue* interviewed Saint Laurent and three of his favorite women: Tina Chow, Paloma Picasso, and de la Falaise wearing his ready-to-wear collection. Under the headline "YVES ONLY!" the piece began with: "Rumors that he was no longer interested, unwell, past his prime, were dispelled by this breathtaking collection, one to rival his greatest." Loulou et al are snapped by Michael Roberts smiling and goofing around, whereas Saint Laurent looks wary in Snowdon's portrait. Nevertheless, he confirms his reputation as the couturier who cares. "I always try to reassure women, even if I am doing a man's suit," he insists. Regarding the expense of couture, he predicts, "Maybe one day things will evolve and there will only be one collection with different prices."

F ashion in the 1980s was full of so many influences; Saint Laurent, on the other hand, continued to bang his own drum and redo versions of his previous hits. "I am sure of myself and my style," he told Mary Russell. "I embroider on the same theme, adding, subtracting, but never deviating from the basic formula." Ultimately, his stubbornness garnered respect from the fashion world. But notwithstanding the occasional "revival of Saint Laurent" article, particularly in the mid-90s when strict tailoring returned, "The Saint's" interminable ready-to-wear shows were not appreciated until he handed over the reins to Alber Elbaz in 1998.

Loulou de la Falaise, Paloma Picasso, and Tina Chow, photographed by Michael Roberts in 1987. In Vogue's "Yves Only" story, each style icon confirms their loyalty to the couturier and adds vivaciousness and glamour to the typically resplendent and stylish Rive Gauche, with de la Falaise's choice of fringe and feathers, Picasso's multihued drama, and Chow's off-the-shoulder chic.

overleaf *The kilt, and tartan, remained successful for Saint Laurent throughout his career. Kate Moss, photographed by Andrew Lamb, wears Rive Gauche in 1994 (left). Saint Laurent frequently used Moss on the runway, and later she became the face of Rive Gauche ready-to-wear and Opium fragrance campaigns. Ludmila Isaeva wears more Rive Gauche tartan (right), with feathered beret and elegant gold-brocade edged black jacket. Photograph by Neil Kirk, 1990.*

The talented Israeli designer injected a modern edge to the Saint Laurent codes. Saint Laurent referred to haute couture as having "multitudes of whispered secrets that a small number of people are still able to pass on," and it was only in couture, and via his Lesage embroidered jackets and sumptuous evening dresses, that he occasionally sparkled with his former magic, bringing to mind his words: "it's perfection of line … it's how to work with a beautiful fabric."

Nevertheless, Saint Laurent's retirement in January 2002 surprised everyone in the fashion world and led to a wave of nostalgia and mild regret. The conference announcing this was held at the couture salon of the avenue Marceau. It was 40 years after his first couture show for his house. Sitting on a small stage, Saint Laurent's hands shook as he read his speech. "Today, I have decided to bid farewell to the world of fashion that I have so loved," he began in touchingly dignified tone. He named individuals who had supported and believed in him. He mentioned Christian Dior and other elements of his career that made him feel proud. "In many ways, I feel that I have created the closet of the contemporary woman and that I have contributed to the transformation of my era." He also took the opportunity to talk about his problems with addiction and depression that had ended in 1991. "I have struggled with anguish and I have been through sheer hell. I have known fear and the terrors of solitude. I have known those fair-weather friends we call tranquilizers and drugs. I have known the prison of depression and the confinement of hospital. But one day, I was able to come through all of that, dazzled yet sober." Once his speech was over, Saint Laurent left, leaving Bergé to answer questions. It was the end of an era, and although the idea led to weeping among intimates, there was also mild relief. Gone was the need to play-act and fib about the "fantasy clothes" that *The Beautiful Fall*'s writer Alicia Drake described as now being "worn by just a handful of women in the world." That world had disappeared to be replaced by an extremely casual one.

Karen Mulder photographed by Tyen smoldering in Saint Laurent's silk crepe hooded couture gown from his 1991 spring/summer collection inspired, said Vogue, by "gentleness" and "soft, creamy fabrics."

previous pages *Entirely Rive Gauche onboard (left), from Elaine Irwin's cotton button-through cropped top and skirt, to her leather drawstring bag. Photograph by Neil Kirk, 1992. Supermodel Carla Bruni wearing a Rive Gauche linen puff-sleeved dress (right), photographed by Kim Knott in 1994.*

Even after retirement, Saint Laurent still went to his studio in the avenue Marceau. He would spend afternoons there, quietly sketching. But such activities ceased when the couture house was made into a museum in 2004. And then Saint Laurent disappeared into the confines of rue de Babylone. To keep him company, there was Moujik no. 4, his stocky French bulldog, house servants, and his prodigious art collection. The rumors around Paris were that he was living a strange, embalmed existence. Saint Laurent had warned that this might be when he had told *Le Figaro*, "Outside of my collections, I live in total absence." It was claimed that the only two activities that tempted him away from watching television were either dining with Betty Catroux, his best friend since 1966, or being driven to a patch of grass on the Champ de Mars where he walked Moujik. However, it actually turned out that, when on form, Saint Laurent would go to Mathis, the private bar-restaurant on rue de Ponthieu, and dine with pals such as Jacques Grange, his former interior decorator. Nor was Saint Laurent averse to going to dinner parties if he knew who else was going to be there.

Supermodel Linda Evangelista photographed by Juergen Teller in 1994 wearing the Rive Gauche Smoking, termed by Vogue a "new wave-tuxedo," displaying the éclat of the modernized classic.

previous pages *Throughout his career, Yves Saint Laurent could be relied upon for immaculate use of white and black and a perfectly cut jacket and pants that made the wearer feel self-assured and protected (left). Photograph by Michel Arnaud, 1982. Saint Laurent's twill trench coat for Rive Gauche (right) exemplifies the timelessness of his designs and illustrates his genius for cut and proportion. Photograph by Barry Lategan, 1971.*

Around 2006, Saint Laurent's arms became paralyzed. Then he had needed a wheelchair owing to a lack of movement in his legs. In spite of his problems, Saint Laurent was cheerful. Convinced that he was on the mend, he told close friends that an elevator would not be necessary in his apartment because he would be shortly able to walk. In fact, Saint Laurent was dying of brain cancer, but Bergé— his constant protector—had decided not to tell him. After bouts in hospital, the 71-year-old Saint Laurent died at his 7th arrondissement home on June 1, 2008. Both Betty Catroux and Bergé were by his side.

His funeral was held at Eglise Saint-Roch, traditionally considered the artist's church, in Paris's 1st arrondissement. Nicolas Sarkozy, the President of the French Republic, attended, accompanied by his wife Carla Bruni-Sarkozy who had often modeled for Saint Laurent.

Designers paying respect included John Galliano, then at Dior, Jean Paul Gaultier, Hubert de Givenchy, Christian Lacroix, Kenzo Takada, Valentino Garavani as well as France's titans of luxury, the magnates Bernard Arnault and François Pinault. Treated like a funeral of state, a French flag was wrapped around the coffin. Outside, on the sidewalk of the rue St. Honoré, a vast crowd had convened to bid farewell to Yves Saint Laurent, France's Giant of Couture. The "vast crowd" made sense because throughout his life, Yves Saint Laurent managed to touch his public on an emotional level—both with his elegant designs and his poetic words. Perhaps it was a mixture of his genius and unusual honesty. Shy as he was when he first exploded on the fashion scene as the boy-wonder successor to Christian Dior, Yves Mathieu-Saint-Laurent, as he was then known, was always strangely direct.

Yves Saint Laurent in his studio, photographed by Snowdon in 1987. In spite of being in his element, fitting a couture frill skirt on Katoucha, a favorite model, the couturier seems vulnerable, an impression he often gave throughout his career.

Saint Laurent was an original, both highly sensitive and witty, who was more inspired by lasting style than fleeting fashion. He often said that all a woman needed to be fashionable was a pair of pants, a sweater, and a trench coat. Pierre Bergé was impressed by Saint Laurent's ability to maintain his sense of childhood and, to quote *Vogue*'s André Leon Talley, "In this utopian inner palace, he could summon memories of his swimming at his family's seaside villa, dressing paper dolls, and putting on a fashion show for his sisters, when he was twelve." Leon Talley was struck by the beauty of Saint Laurent's tapered fingers, which reminded him of "a Renaissance aristocrat in a Bronzino." Yet he will be best remembered as rendering every type of women beautiful. "It is by perfecting essential items of clothing—a marvelous position—that I created my style," Saint Laurent said. It was a philosophy that infused his designs and confirmed his preeminent place in fashion history.

"Without elegance of heart, there is no elegance."

YVES SAINT LAURENT

Index

Page numbers in *italic* refer to illustrations

References

Benaïm, Laurence *Yves Saint Laurent*, Editions Grasset et Fasquelle, 1993

Benaïm, Laurence *Debut, Yves Saint Laurent 1962*, Harry N Abrams, 2002

Bergé, Pierre *Yves Saint Laurent*, Thames & Hudson, 1997

Bergé, Pierre *10 Ans, Fondation Pierre Bergé, Yves Saint Laurent*, Editions du Regard, 2014

Drake, Alicia *The Beautiful Fall: Fashion, Genius and Glorious Excess in 1970s Paris*, Bloomsbury, 2006

Dupire, Beatrice and Sy, Hady (eds) *Yves Saint Laurent: Forty Years of Creation 1958–1998*, International Festival of Fashion Photography, 1998

Fraser-Cavassoni, Natasha *Monsieur Dior: Once Upon A Time*, Pointed Leaf Press, 2014

Müller, Florence and Bowles, Hamish *Yves Saint Laurent, Style, Style, Style*, Abrams, 2008

De Ravenel, Ariel and Fraser-Cavassoni, Natasha *Loulou de la Falaise*, Rizzoli, 2014

Rawsthorn, Alice *Yves Saint Laurent: A Biography*, HarperCollins, 1996

Sinclair Charlotte *Vogue on Christian Dior*, Quadrille, 2012

Vreeland, Diana *DV*, George Weidenfeld & Nicholson, 1984

Vreeland, Diana (ed) *Yves Saint Laurent*, The Metropolitan Museum of Art and Clarkson Potter, 1983

Picture credits

Acknowledgments

First and foremost, I have to thank Alexandra Shulman and Harriet Wilson at *Vogue* as well as Jane O'Shea at Quadrille for making it possible for me to write about Yves Saint Laurent. It's impossible to celebrate Saint Laurent's illustrious career without mentioning Pierre Bergé, his business partner and keeper of the flame. *Mille mercis* to Monsieur Bergé and his team at the Fondation Pierre Bergé—Yves Saint Laurent: Philippe Mugnier, Laetitia Roux, Pascal Sittler, Pauline Vidal, and Olivier Flaviano who proved to be both enthusiastic and accommodating. Once again, I relied upon Perrine Scherrer from Dior's archives, an excellent source for Saint Laurent's debut years. I also acknowledge Dior's Jérôme Gautier—my favorite fashion photographic encyclopedia—who proved invaluable for recognizing and naming *Vogue* models. *Vogue* article and image research was greatly eased by Condé Nast's Brett Croft and Ben Evans. I was in touch with Ben daily and he became a guardian angel for his enthusiasm, knowledge, and politeness. At Quadrille, I worked with Nicola Ellis and Gemma Hayden and felt extremely grateful for their patience and savoir-faire. Writing means rewriting and I was fortunate to have the editing skills of Sarah Mitchell who always encouraged. The latter also applies to my agents Ed Victor and Maggie Phillips. When delving into Saint Laurent, it was difficult not to quote from *The Beautiful Fall* by Alicia Drake. She is a dear friend and her book remains an inspired reference to Saint Laurent's life and career. I also called upon the help of Madison Cox, a stalwart ally, on two separate occasions. Finally, it was thanks to my mother Antonia Fraser that I discovered Saint Laurent's Rive Gauche and indeed *Vogue*. Both elements fueled my childhood and brought me a life in Paris.

Publishing Consultant Jane O'Shea
Creative Director Helen Lewis
Series Editor Sarah Mitchell
Series Designer Nicola Ellis
Designer Gemma Hayden
Production Director Vincent Smith
Production Controller Emily Noto

For *Vogue*:
Commissioning Editor Harriet Wilson
Picture Researcher Ben Evans

First published in 2015 by
Quadrille Publishing Limited
Pentagon House
52–54 Southwark Street
London SE1 1UN
www.quadrille.co.uk

Quadrille is an imprint of Hardie Grant
www.hardiegrant.com.au

Text copyright © 2015 Condé Nast
Publications Limited.
Vogue Regd TM is owned by the Condé Nast
Publications Ltd and is used under licence
from it. All rights reserved.
Design and Layout © 2013 Quadrille
Publishing Limited.

Library of Congress Control Number:
2014959345

ISBN: 978-1-4197-1801-4

Published in 2015 by Abrams Image, an
imprint of ABRAMS. All rights reserved.
No portion of this book may be reproduced,
stored in a retrieval system, or transmitted
in any form or by any means, mechanical,
electronic, photocopying, recording, or
otherwise, without written permission from
the publisher.

Printed and bound in China
10 9 8 7 6 5 4 3 2 1

Abrams Image books are available at special
discounts when purchased in quantity
for premiums and promotions as well as
fundraising or educational use. Special
editions can also be created to specification.
For details, contact specialsales@
abramsbooks.com or the address below.

ABRAMS
THE ART OF BOOKS SINCE 1949

115 West 18th Street
New York, NY 10011
www.abramsbooks.com